HEAVEN BEGUILES THE TIRED

THOMAS W. FORD

HEAVEN
BEGUILES
THE TIRED

DEATH IN THE POETRY OF EMILY DICKINSON

UNIVERSITY OF ALABAMA PRESS
University, Alabama

To Pete and Tommy
and another Emily

Contents

❖

Acknowledgments

❖

As will be obvious to the reader, I owe a great debt to a number of previous writers, but most especially to Emily Dickinson's principal biographers and interpreters, George Frisbie Whicher, Richard Chase, Millicent Todd Bingham, Thomas H. Johnson, and Charles R. Anderson, whose works have been constant sources of information, guidance, and inspiration. For the ideas I received from the many articles by many authors, I also make grateful acknowledgment.

I am especially grateful to Professor Philip Graham for his encouragement, counsel, and advice. I wish to thank the following people who, either recently or years ago, either directly or indirectly, contributed to the shaping of this book: Professors George Williams, William S. Dix, Mody C. Boatright, and Joseph J. Jones. I thank my wife, Cora L. Ford, for her careful reading of the manuscript.

I wish to thank John C. Guilds, head of the Department of English at the University of South Carolina, for his aid and interest.

For permission to quote from the poems and letters of Emily Dickinson, grateful acknowledgment is made to the following:

By permission of the publishers and the Trustees of Amherst College from Thomas H. Johnson, Editor, *The Poems of Emily Dickinson*, Cambridge, Mass.: The Belknap Press of Harvard University Press, Copyright, 1951, 1955, by The President and Fellows of Harvard College.

By permission of the publishers from Thomas H. Johnson and Theodora V. W. Ward (Eds.), *The Letters of Emily Dickinson*, Cambridge, Mass.: The Belknap Press of Harvard University Press, Copyright, 1958, by The President and Fellows of Harvard College.

By permission of Houghton Mifflin Company from Martha Dickinson Bianchi, *The Life and Letters of Emily Dickinson*, © 1924.

By permission of Little, Brown & Company from Thomas H. Johnson (Ed.), *The Complete Poems of Emily Dickinson*. Copyright 1914, 1935, 1942, © 1963 by Martha Dickinson Bianchi; copyright 1929, © 1957 by Mary L. Hampson.

Grateful acknowledgment for permission to quote is also made to the following:

Charles Scribner's Sons: from George F. Whicher, *This Was a Poet*, © 1938.

Harper & Row: from Millicent Todd Bingham and Mabel Loomis Todd, editors, *Bolts of Melody*, © 1945, and from Millicent Todd Bingham, *Emily Dickinson's Home*, © 1955.

Harvard University Press: from Theodore Spencer, *Death and Elizabethan Tragedy*, © 1936, and from Thomas H. Johnson, *Emily Dickinson: An Interpretive Biography*, © 1955.

Holt, Rinehart & Winston: from Charles R. Anderson, *Emily Dickinson's Poetry: Stairway of Surprise*, © 1960.

Vanguard Press: from Ralph Barton Perry, *Puritanism and Democracy*, © 1944.

William Sloane Associates: from Richard Chase, *Emily Dickinson*, © 1951.

Brief portions of this book, in somewhat modified form, first appeared as articles in *The Midwest Quarterly* (October, 1962) and in *The University Review* (March, 1965). I thank the editors for kindly granting their permission to use this material here.

Preface

❖

WHEN A MAJOR POET GIVES EMPHATIC ATtention to a single theme over a period of many years, the reader feels an urgent desire to ask: Why? In this book, as the subtitle indicates, the preoccupied poet is Emily Dickinson, the persistent topic is death.

Emily Dickinson's intense interest in this subject has often been noted, but has not been explored completely and in depth. Before 1955, to be sure, the full extent and intensity of her concern could only be surmised, since it was known that a number of her poems remained unpublished and there was no generally accepted chronology for the poems that were in print. Under these conditions, no one could know to what extent Emily Dickinson's interest in death represented a life-long preoccupation, and no one could know the quality of her concern at different stages in her development.

This state of affairs was radically altered in 1955, however, with the publication of Thomas H. Johnson's *The Poems of Emily Dickinson*, an invaluable work that provides reliable texts for all the poems known to

have been written by Emily Dickinson, and which es-
tablishes a plausible chronology for most of them.
Among other things, it shows conclusively that death
was a theme of major importance at every stage of
Emily Dickinson's creative development, and that at
no time was her interest merely frivolous.

Much of Emily Dickinson's poetry on death reveals
a markedly existentialist view. To label her an "existentialist", of course, would perform the disservice of any
generality. One can find elements of this eclectic philosophy in almost any writing, if he looks long enough. It
is undeniable, however, that in her preoccupation with
doubt, time, despair, and the separation of man from
nature; in her anxiety, ambiguity, revolt from tradition; and especially in her preference for the concrete
rather than the abstract, she anticipated some of the
concerns that were later to figure prominently in existential thought.

If one sees her quest for the concrete as focusing on
and ending in death; if one views her inner tension,
anguish, and anxiety as akin to the German *Angst*, then
it is meaningful to call attention to her existentialist
attitude. Reality for her was not to be trapped in abstractions. Passionately aware of her role as an individual existing in time, with care and concern (Heidegger's *Sorge*) she directed her poetic thought on the
crucial experience of death.

Her concern with death was not morbid and it was
not Romantic. She lived in separation and in tension,
and she did not rest comfortably in the "sure-enwind-
ing arms of cool-enfolding death", as did Walt Whit-

man. She was totally and urgently engaged in her poetic
investigation of death, living and reliving the mystery
of death in all its ambiguities, and finding in the ambiguities of death the ambiguities of life.

Emily Dickinson's philosophy was in fact no philosophy—certainly she had no "system" and was not given
to any belief in "Pure Thought". There was nothing
of the Hegelian in her—and in this, again, she was unlike Whitman. For her, the idea of immortality was not
to be grasped as an abstraction, but was to be conceived
only by comparison to concrete sensation. And even
this kind of "heaven" was conditional—a heaven *if* true.
Still further, her recognition of the limitations of the
mind allowed her to perceive the charm *and* deceit
inherent in abstractions, allowed her to know poetically
that "Heaven beguiles the tired".

If the present study has a central thesis it is, in essence, that Emily Dickinson's intense interest in death
was the most important single factor in shaping the
contours of her poetry. This is not to say that it was
the only important factor, of course, for it most certainly was not. But among the several more important
formative influences that are discernible in Emily Dickinson's poems, her preoccupation with death was, I con-
tend, the most powerful and the most enduring. I have
attempted to demonstrate the force of this influence, to
uncover the basic reasons for its being so important,
and finally, by analysis of her major poems on the subject, to reveal something of the function and significance of death in her poetry—and in her life.

Thomas W. Ford

HEAVEN BEGUILES THE TIRED

5449

Emily Dickinson's Attitude Toward Death

❖

THERE IS NOTHING EXTRAORDINARY IN THE fact that Emily Dickinson wrote many poems concerned with death. It is a venerable theme, on which a great body of literature has been written. There is something exceptional, however, in the fact that so large a part of her work deals with the subject. Nearly all of the major Dickinson critics have noted the importance of the death theme to her poetry. George Frisbie Whicher, for example, says that "she recurred to it [the subject of death] more frequently than to any other". Richard Chase comments that "in the large majority of Emily Dickinson's poems, from the least impressive to the most, there are intimations of death". Thomas H. Johnson, while recognizing that many poets have made death central in much of their poetry, also believes that "Emily Dickinson did so in hers to an unusual degree". Charles R. Anderson writes that death and immortality were "the two profoundest themes that challenged her poetic powers". The frequency and importance of the theme indicate that a full study is clearly warranted.[1]

The subject is not restricted to any one period but appears throughout her creative work. As her niece Martha Dickinson Bianchi noted, Emily Dickinson was "eternally preoccupied with death".[2] In a similar vein, the editors of *Bolts of Melody* state:

> From the time when Emily Dickinson first began to write poetry until her last fading pencil marks on tattered bits of paper, the mystery of death absorbed her.[3]

Her letters also abound with references to death, and confirm the fact that her preoccupation with the subject was a lifelong one. In a letter to T. W. Higginson, February, 1863, she commented on her early awareness of death: "Perhaps Death—gave me awe for friends—striking sharp and early, for I held them since—in a brittle love—of more alarm, than peace" (II, 423).[4] Her chronic consciousness of death continued unabated throughout her life. Less than a month before her death she wrote: "There is no Trumpet like the Tomb" (III, 904).

Though there were many possible reasons for her great concern with death, at the heart of her preoccupation was a religious motivation.[5] She could neither embrace nor abandon the prickly matter of religious faith. The very fact that she was the only member of her immediate family who was never to join a church is perhaps evidence of the seriousness with which she approached religion: having felt no inner conversion, she could not honestly acknowledge allegiance to a church. This refusal was very likely a source of self–doubt and torment, but a burden perhaps made easier to bear through her poetry.[6]

Emily Dickinson often dealt in her poems with what are conventionally termed "spiritual values". A casual glance through her poems and letters reveals numerous allusions to such subjects as eternity, immortality, time, infinity, God, and resurrection. Because she was deeply concerned with religious values, she was equally anxious to investigate every attitude towards death. It may be that Man's ability to foresee death is at the core of religion in general; certainly Emily Dickinson saw the two as closely related.

A letter of 1850, written at the age of twenty to her friend Abiah Root, illustrates the association of death and religion in Emily's mind. Expressing grief over the death of Leonard Humphrey, one of her early "preceptors", Emily wrote:

> . . . there must be much to hope for, but when the un-reconciled spirit has nothing left but God, that spirit is lone indeed. I don't think there will be any sun-shine, or any singing–birds in the spring that's com-ing. . . . I will try not to say any more—my rebellious thoughts are many, and the friend I love and trust in has much *now* to forgive.   (I, 103)

Aware that her religious thoughts are unorthodox and "rebellious", she implied that, if she were a believing Christian, she would accept the death of her friend calmly, receiving consolation from the immortality promised by Christianity. She ended her letter with a remark indicating that her inability to accept death stoically might very well have a religious drawback:

> You are growing wiser than I am, and nipping in the bud fancies which I let blossom—perchance to bear no fruit, or if plucked, I may find it bitter. . . . You are learning control and firmness. Christ Jesus will love you more. I'm afraid he don't love me *any*!
>
> (I, 104)

In a letter written to Mrs. J. G. Holland in 1856, Emily, then twenty–six, implied that religion is necessary only because death is present in the world:

> If roses had not faded, and frosts had never come, and one had not fallen here and there whom I could not waken, there were no need of other Heaven than the one below.   (II, 329)

One of the major reasons for her interest in death, then, was its close association with religion, as she viewed it. The relationship between death and religion became for her, in fact, a circular one. Doubts concerning traditionally held religious beliefs focused her attention on death. Intense awareness of death prompted religious concern. The two were mutually reinforcing. Cause became effect; effect became cause. A process was established that provided its own fuel.

Did Emily Dickinson believe in immortality? Since her concern with death was, at least in part, religiously motivated, to determine what her belief was is highly important. A close scrutiny of death seems frequently to give rise to the question of a life after death.[7] The zeal to prove physically the reality of immortality was prevalent among many of Emily Dickinson's contemporaries. Hamlin Garland, William Dean Howells, and Sarah Whitman all exhibited such desire to an extreme degree. Emily Dickinson's anxious search, however, took a somewhat different form. She was not, for example, actually interested in spiritualism, as Howells was in *The Undiscovered Country*.

One who wished to prove that Emily Dickinson had a positive intimation of immortality would have little difficulty selecting poems and letters to support his belief. The following poems, probably written between her twenty-eighth and thirty-fifth years, are examples. In "I never saw a moor—" (II, 1052)[8] she announced positively her feeling with respect to the existence of heaven. A belief in resurrection is expressed in "Adrift! A little boat adrift!" (I, 30). In "Ambition cannot find him" (I, 68) she indicated that those who were undistinguished in life would become eminent through immortality. That the dead will live again in heaven is implied in "Those fair—fictitious People—" (II, 499), and evidence of a belief in immortality is readily discernible in "Conscious am I in my Chamber" (II, 679) and "It is an honorable Thought" (II, 946).

Certain letters at various intervals over the years support this view. In 1863, at age thirty-three, she expressed her hope of immortality in a letter to T. W. Higginson (II, 424). In a letter of 1879, Emily, then forty-nine, offered help to her cousin whose young daughter had died: " 'Come unto me' could not alarm those minute feet—how sweet to remember" (II, 648). In a letter of 1881 the poet consoled Mrs. J. G. Holland on the death of her husband by stating that he had achieved immortality (III, 713).

These examples are misleading, however, and do not prove that Emily Dickinson was firmly convinced of immortality. One senses a strained quality in her affirmations, as if she desperately wanted to believe but could not honestly do so unreservedly. Furthermore, evidence on the other side strongly indicates that her basic feelings about immortality were ones of doubt and apprehension.[9] Certain poems evince this attitude clearly.

"I know that He exists" (I, 338), written when she was about thirty-two, begins by suggesting that perhaps God remains silent merely to make bliss seem the more rewarding when it is finally achieved; the silence is a whim, an "instant's play" of His nature. The poem concludes, however, with a note of anxiety: what if the "play" proved to be earnest? What if death were the end? The jest would then have been carried too far. In sum, the poem expresses just the opposite of the notion that immortality is a certainty.

That the chances for immortality are at best tenuous is the viewpoint of "Not probable—The barest Chance—" (I, 346). The soul may be only next door to paradise, and then, "A smile too few—a word too much", and immortality is missed. Man is, indeed, in a precarious position. "Heaven is so far of the Mind" (I, 370) implies that paradise is only in the mind and that immortality may be only a concept of the mind, vanishing when the mind vanishes.

No poem expresses her doubt more clearly than "Which is best? Heaven—" (II, 1012), written when she was about thirty–five. The heaven to come always bears "that old Codicil of Doubt". The poet has the haunting fear that heaven may be in the opposite direction from where she has been looking. The poem, "A loss of something ever felt I—" (II, 959), expresses the dread suspicion that she will never find the "Kingdom of Heaven". In her forty–third year, she wrote of a conditional heaven in "That Heaven if we achieve" (III, 1258).

In fact, the poem conjectures, can anyone ever be certain of his immortality? The sage knows no more of immortality than you or I, and even the bravest men die "ignorant of their resumption" (III, 1497). In "Their Hight [sic] in Heaven comforts not—" (II, 696) the implication is that, because the poet is finite, heaven is beyond her vision and is only supposition. Judging from evidence, all one can say is, "I dont know".

This same tone of doubt and insecurity regarding immortality is prevalent in her letters. Writing at twenty–three to Dr. and Mrs. J. G. Holland, she suddenly changed her statement to a question: "Heaven is large —is it not? Life is short too, isn't it? Then when one is done, is there not another?" (I, 264). There is no positive conviction here, but a questioning. Similarly, in a letter written to her sister, Lavinia, in 1860, she won-

dered whether her aunt who had recently died would
be able to "look down" on them, and "if she sees us
now, if she sees *me*, who said that she 'loved Emily' "
(II, 362).

The death of Emily Dickinson's father in June, 1874,
was a great blow. If she had any real convictions of immortality, now, if ever, would be the time to call upon
them for solace—but she does not do so. At forty–four,
she wrote to her cousins about taking flowers to his
grave, remarking how comforting it would be, "if we
only knew he knew" (II, 526). Two years later she
wrote the cousins that much of her time was occupied
with "wondering where he is" (II, 559). At fifty–two
she wrote to them in similar vein, following the death
of her mother in 1882: "We don't know where she is,
though so many tell us" (III, 750).

Referring to the death of a mutual friend, Emily
Dickinson commented to Maria Whitney, in a letter
of 1879, that while they could not help each other to
believe, one might *hope* that God, in whatever form,
would be true to the friend. Characteristically, she rejected the possibility that human beings could ever be
certain of immortality: "Consciousness is the only home
of which we *now* know" (II, 634).

Quantitatively, the amount of evidence supporting
the view that Emily Dickinson had great doubt and
anxiety regarding immortality is far larger than that
supporting the view that she felt a positive conviction
of an afterlife.[10] Qualitatively, the poems and letters expressing anxiety seem to have a truer ring than those ex-

pressing certainty and positive conviction. Her sense of anxiety and doubt, the view that man is in a rather precarious position in an unfriendly universe was influential in shaping the basic contours of her poetry.[11]

This unstable position between acceptance and rejection, ending in anxiety, when joined with her instinctive fondness for household imagery, opens an avenue toward valid generalizations about her art.

The high value of Emily Dickinson's contributions to creative literature is firmly established. But to see orphic wisdom in everything she wrote, to see profound metaphysical speculations in her poetry, will only obscure the real worth of her writings. She was not basically an abstract thinker. On the contrary, she was conditioned by her great love for her home to think in "household" terms. Her acute observation of the rather limited view of nature that she received from her garden likewise influenced the character of her thought, as did her knowledge of village life. The abstract concepts of Time, Eternity, Infinity, and Immortality forced themselves upon her thinking by way of her intense personal concern with religious matters and her anxieties about a possible future life after death. But her response to these ideas was expressed in terms of her familiar surroundings.[12]

Much of the peculiar freshness, individuality, and power of her writing may be attributed to her ability to juxtapose the concrete with the abstract, the homey with the heavenly, the housefly with eternity. It also partly explains why some readers insist on seeing profound metaphysical truths in all she wrote. Actually, however, the ideas that are highlighted and made exceptionally vivid in her poetry might well be dismissed as rather conventional if expressed in prose. One might justly claim, of course, that her very manner of expression itself constitutes profundity. Emily Dickinson certainly was not void of ideas; to the contrary, she was a serious and enlightened thinker. But to assert that she was a philosopher in the full sense of that term is a disservice, for this can only cloud efforts to assess her value as something perhaps better than a mere philosopher—her value as a poet.

Emily Dickinson was not a well–organized thinker, and any attempt to infer a carefully arranged, well–ordered, coherent system from her poems must be fruitless.[13] No such system exists. By her own admission, she had difficulty in organizing her thoughts. She wrote to T. W. Higginson: "I had no Monarch in my life, and cannot rule myself, and when I try to organize— my little Force explodes—and leaves me bare and charred" (II, 414).

Though the poetry of Emily Dickinson is highly individual, it does not seem especially original in either literal ideas or figurative images *per se*, and was not so even in her own time. In her descriptions of death, for example, *cold* is perhaps the most frequently used adjective. Frost and snow are persistent symbols for death: "Delayed till in it's [*sic*][14] vest of snow/ Her loving bosom lay" (I, 58); "This Bird—observing others/ When frosts too sharp became" (I, 148); "The Frost—possess the World—/ In Cabinets—be shown" (II, 517); "Two Travellers perishing in Snow" (II, 933); "Snow beneath whose chilly softness/ Some that never lay" (II, 942); "Too cold is this/ To warm with Sun—/ Too stiff to bended be" (II, 1135); and "A further afternoon to fail/ As Flower at fall of Frost" (III, 1667). The association of death with cold is certainly not original. Theodore Spencer, in his convincing book on the complex and important role of death in Elizabethan drama (*Death and Elizabethan Tragedy*, Cambridge, 1936), points out that *cold* was one of the five adjectives most commonly applied to death in the popular literature of the fourteenth and fifteenth centuries.[15]

Emily Dickinson's earliest dated poem, written in 1850, contains a line, "death claims a living bride" (I, 1). Death associated with brides, bridegrooms, or weddings appears in several of her poems. In the poem beginning "A Wife—at Daybreak I shall be" (I, 461), the implication is that the poet will be a wife, but only after death. A similar conjunction occurs in "Given in Marriage unto Thee/ Oh thou Celestial Host" (II, 817). In "Title divine—is mine" (II, 1072) she is "Born—Bridalled—Shrouded" in a single day. "Death is the supple Suitor" (III, 1445) clearly reveals death as a lover and as a bridegroom. Death carries on a courtship: "It is a stealthy Wooing", carried on cautiously at first. At last, death becomes bold and enters with bugles and a coach and "bears away in triumph/ To troth unknown". Again, the association is a very old one, found in the Greek Anthology, in Shakespeare (*King Lear, Antony and Cleopatra, Measure for Measure*), and other venerable sources.[16]

Death as a king, a monarch, a tyrant, or some kind of royalty appears frequently in her poetry. Death will supply coach, footmen, and dignified attendants: "None can avoid this purple—/ None evade this Crown" (I, 98). "Triumph—may be of several Kinds" (I, 455) refers to death as "that Old Imperator". Again, death is a "Despot" and "the King of Down" (III, 1334). Death is also a "King" in the poem, "I heard a Fly buzz—when I died" (I, 465). As Theodore Spencer again points out, this image was much used in Elizabethan drama, appearing in works by Marlowe, Marston, and Shakespeare.[17]

Death associated with sleep, night, or darkness, also appears often in Emily Dickinson's poetry: "There's something quieter than sleep/ Within this inner room" (I, 45), and "A long—long Sleep—A famous Sleep—/ That makes no show for Morn" (II, 654). She refers to death as "Night's possibility" (I, 106) and relates noon to life, and night to death in "As plan for Noon and plan for Night" (II, 960). She associates death with the sunset: "For I wear the 'Thorns, till *Sunset*/ Then—my Diadem put on" (III, 1737). Death and sleep are associated hundreds of times by classic authors.[18]

Death as a democrat, an equalizer, a leveler appears in her poetry, and the image is, for example, central to the poem, "Color—Caste—Denomination—/ These are Time's Affair" (II, 970). Death does not hold to this clas-

sification, and his "large—Democratic fingers/ Rub
away the Brand". Again the image appears in "Not any
higher stands the Grave/ For Heroes than for Men"
(III, 1256). The child and the old man, "The Beggar
and his Queen/ Propitiate this Democrat". This identification, too, is venerable, making a frequent appearance throughout the history of the Dances of Death
—those rather grotesque allegorical representations
prominent in the Middle Ages, by which Christians of
every station were reminded that death is ultimately
faced by all humanity. Death was frequently depicted as
a skeleton leading other skeletons or the living to the
grave. Paintings, poems, or carvings were used in cemeteries and cloisters, and the figure of death appeared in
many forms. The Dance of Death (*Danse Macabre*) was
also enacted in morality plays. Apparently, in both the
pictorial presentations and the explanatory poems, the
fact that death would treat all alike was clearly por-
trayed.[19] Death leveled all inequalities; the king, the
peasant, the sage, the fool, the murderer, the saint, the
atheist, the pope—all must dance in its procession.[20]

Often enough Emily Dickinson equated death with
parting or separation: "We'll pass without the parting"
(II, 996); "The Auctioneer of Parting" (III, 1612);
and "My life closed twice before its close" (III, 1732).
Here again we may see echoes from Elizabethan literature, such as the several Shakespearean sonnets in which
the absence theme is treated.

The personification of death is common in Emily
Dickinson's poetry—as it was in the Dances of Death.

It was also in general use in Elizabethan drama.[21] Other
concepts of death found in both the poetry of Emily
Dickinson and in Elizabethan drama are the following:
death as a comforter, as one offering rest and security;
death as a traveler; the vanity and transiency of life as
contrasted with the permanency of death. Devices common to both were the use of church bells, tombs, graveyards, and funerals.

The point is that Emily Dickinson's particular skill
did not lie in the originality, as such, of her ideas or
images—but this fact is not to her discredit! Few would
deny the contribution made by Elizabethan drama, and
yet the concepts cited above were no more original with
the Elizabethans than they were with Emily Dickinson.
Theodore Spencer points out that Elizabethan drama
"uses nearly all the ideas about death that had been
passed on to it from the past".[22] It should not be supposed that Emily Dickinson necessarily borrowed her
ideas or images from the Elizabethans or, for that matter, from any of her reading. More than likely, of the
sources mentioned above, she was probably familiar
only with Shakespeare. As George Whicher observes,
"Emily Dickinson's poetry is not derivable from her
reading".[23] Where, then, did the thoughts come from?
They appear to be among the common stock of ideas
and images that may well suggest themselves to almost
any sensitive poet who has occasion to think seriously
about death. Transmuted into Emily Dickinson's poetry, however, these concepts—and even clichés—be-

came converted reflections of her own divergent views on death. Her special talent was for the union, the co-alition of idea and image in poetic context.

On April 25, 1862, Emily wrote to T. W. Higginson, telling him, "I sing, as the Boy does by the Burying Ground—because I am afraid" (II, 404). The conjecture usually set forth to explain these words is that her fear was caused by her knowledge that the Reverend Charles Wadsworth was leaving Philadelphia for San Francisco.[24] But must it be assumed that she intended so specific a reference? Could it not be merely a statement of her general awareness and fear of death? One naturally associates the words "burying ground" with death. Whatever the case, she was plainly saying here that she was writing poetry because she was afraid; and if the above interpretation is accepted, she wrote to relieve the tensions created by her great concern with death. As Thomas H. Johnson says, Emily Dickinson's poetry was one of "the means by which she relieved her apprehensions".[25]

Death was one of the central problems of her life, and she was to approach it in her poetry from every avenue that occurred to her.[26] She became an "observer" of death—and its effects on the living—as witnessed in her immediate family, in nature, in neighboring houses—giving special attention to such things as funerals and "busy" household activities in houses recently visited by death. Though she realized early that no final revelation of immortality was to come in this life, as indicated by the concluding lines of a poem written in 1858,

". . . within the Riddle/ One will walk today" (I, 50), the actual physical process of dying was nonetheless the last observable link in which she might find some hint of immortality, and she could never refrain from observing.[27]

Emily Dickinson felt great anxiety about death, but in many ways she was realistic in her recognition that for her, at least, this very anxiety was a major problem in itself. She apparently did not try to escape the problem by ignoring it, or by accepting some secondhand or easy solution. Rejecting pre–conceptions, she chose to pursue that first–hand experience of the existentialist. She tried to become as familiar as possible with death in all its aspects, in the hope that when she did come face to face with it, the experience would not be wholly unfamiliar. In this sense, it might be said that life for her was a preparation for death. She writes:

> I made my soul familiar—with her extremity—
> That at the last, it should not be a novel Agony—
> But she, and Death, acquainted—
> Meet tranquilly, as friends—
> Salute, and pass, without a Hint—
> And there, the Matter ends—   (I, 412)

Thus, in an effort to face death Emily Dickinson, through her poetry, tried to make its acquaintance.[28] She had no single guiding "philosophy of death". Moving around the circumference, gazing at death in the center, she saw its many faces, each evoking from her a different emotional response. In its presence she was by turns coy, impertinent, fearful, awed, reverent, friendly, resentful.[29]

Her deficiencies as an original or systematic thinker might have led to mediocre philosophy,[30] but in point of fact led to good poetry. If she had been more consistent and well–organized she still might have written poetry, and even poetry of some value, but it would have been poetry of a different kind. The instability and inconsistency of her ideas about death imparted conflict, tension, and drama to her writings. As a close observer, she could not deny to herself the overwhelming truth and reality of death as an unmistakable fact. Yet fears and hopes prompted by religion caused her to dwell on the possibility of there being *something* in store even after physical death. The outcome, in her poetry, was the intermingling of concrete household terms, images taken from her immediate environment, and whatever abstract concepts of death she was forced to dwell upon as a result of her religious trouble.

Death gave her poetry a universal subject matter, and she blended in the homey, concrete images with which she was familiar. It is this fusion of idea and image, of the concrete with the abstract, of sensation with thought that is her particular contribution. Her juxtaposition of the impertinent with the reverent, the familiar with the strange, is almost an identifying characteristic of her poetry.[31]

These observations are neither new nor startling. Critics have frequently pointed them out. Allen Tate long ago gave emphasis to the fact that Emily Dickinson was a poet and not a metaphysician, and pointed to her identifying characteristic of presenting the abstract in terms of sensation. Later critics, whether at-

Biographical Influences

❖

To understand the death poetry of
Emily Dickinson, one must consider the particular cir-
cumstances of her life and environment that shaped her
attitude. This is not to say that one should seek out particular personal experiences that may be reflected in
the poetry. The fictive "I" in her poetry is, as she said,
a "supposed person". But this transmuted personal experience, dramatized in her poetry, must have had some
shaping influence. One such influence, long recognized
by biographers and critics, was her Puritan background.

The response she made to her Puritan past—and thus
its effect on her—cannot be stated in terms of simple
affirmation or denial. It is more subtle, more puzzling
than a simple yes-or-no response. Certain traditions she
rejected—and yet was haunted by that "old Codicil of
Doubt" even as she did so. No actual Puritan theocracy
existed during her lifetime, of course, but Emily Dickinson's Amherst was still very much under the influence

of its Puritan tradition. Amherst College, founded in 1821 largely through the efforts of her grandfather, was established mainly to train its men in orthodox Christian views and send them into the world as preachers or teachers. Emily's father and brother were both active in college affairs, and she was reared in an atmosphere of strict Christian thinking.

Thomas H. Johnson has pointed out that by the eighteenth century the religious life of the Boston area had become somewhat more urbane than before, with less emphasis on doctrinal niceties.[1] Such was emphatically not the case, however, in the Connecticut Valley region, where earlier Solomon Stoddard had been the most influential promulgator of Christian orthodoxy. While Stoddard had relaxed restrictions on church membership, allowing all who wished to receive God's "grace" to join (not merely those who already were considered, or who considered themselves, members of the "elect"), his grandson and chosen successor, Jonathan Edwards, re–emphasized God's absolute authority and abandoned his grandfather's comparatively liberal policy on church membership. Edwards also laid great stress on the importance of a constant seeking after God's grace, on a constant effort for conversion—that is, on not limiting the religious conscience to the Sabbath alone. Edwards' influence was still felt in Amherst in Emily Dickinson's day. As Johnson describes it:

> . . . the Calvinistic tradition ran deep for all, and the need to focus upon self–improvement and the soul's affections was basic. From the days of Solomon Stod-

> dard the Valley had been unique in one respect. It had
> seen many revival harvests conducted by preachers
> . . . . Outpourings of spirit were traditional with the
> communities, and a part of every family's experience.
> For an individual not to undergo conversion by physi-
> cal sensation was almost a moral delinquency.[2]

It is clear that Emily Dickinson must have been under great social pressure to receive conversion, and yet
she could not bring herself to make the required formal
declaration of faith. There is reason to believe that she
was troubled by this fact even at an early age. In a letter
of January, 1846, she expressed her worry over the matter, indicating that she was just on the point of "accepting" Christ but had drifted back into her old ways (I,
27). She also stated that she was conscious of the "sin"
in her not freely accepting Christ's mercy.

Though never actually a member of a church, Emily
Dickinson continued to attend services rather regularly
until probably around 1852, after which time her at-
tendance became less and less frequent, and finally
stopped entirely. She could not accept the orthodoxies
of her religious environment.[3]

She was never a careful student of Puritan theology
and was unfamiliar with many of its doctrinal and metaphysical subtleties. However, there appear to be certain
general Puritan attitudes that quite likely were accepted
in her own day, and which may throw some light on her
attitude toward death. According to Ralph Barton
Perry, "A highly saturated Puritan life is marked by its
preoccupation with religion".[4] "Preoccupation" does

not necessarily mean "obsession" but, more accurately, that religion is the most fundamental interest of the Puritan, influencing and coloring all other matters, not only on the Sabbath but throughout the week. Emily Dickinson, though unorthodox in her religion, could write: "Some keep the Sabbath going to Church—/ I keep it, staying at Home" (I, 324), and her conclusion was: "So instead of getting to Heaven, at last—/ I'm going, all along". Religion, thoughts on eternity and immortality were never very distant from her mind, but always hovering close by. The poet could write that eternity was not "there", but something very near, sharing her house and joining her in her walks: "No Friend have I that so persists/ As this Eternity" (III, 1684).

Another idea basic to Puritan thinking was the belief that hardship and pain in this life should be stoically endured in order to achieve salvation in the next. The Puritans emphasized the desirability of renunciation of worldly fame and fortune, of bearing the burdens of pain and privation in this life to assure acceptance in the next, of purifying the soul through struggle and endurance here "on earth". Their credo was essentially that of Bunyan's allegory in *The Pilgrim's Progress*.

The belief in purificaton through hardship is frequently evinced in Emily Dickinson's poetry. By reading about others who have borne up under burdens, we are strengthened "Till we—are stouter—/ What they —renounced—/ Till we—are less afraid" (I, 260). The idea of the struggling soul is explicit in "Soul, Wilt thou toss again?" (I, 139). Though many have been lost, a few have gained "an all", and angels are waiting in heaven to "record thee" on the ballot. The struggle with one's own soul is the most important of all battles fought: "Of all the Battles prevalent—/ By far the Greater One—" (II, 594). The path to God is not easy, and the road is often rough; God will lead his chosen "Oftener through Realm of Briar/ Than the Meadow mild" (II, 1021).

Puritan thought also emphasized the idea of salvation through a personal experience of conversion, of receiving grace, of being chosen as one of the members of God's elect. As Perry says, grace could be known only "by him who tastes it for himself".[5] It could not be demonstrated through reason or rules. Only the individual himself could know whether he had truly received God's love. For one who sincerely believed in this test and yet knew that he had not experienced a conversion, the anxiety could be intense to the point of anguish. Strict Puritanism, for those who had not received "grace", could indeed cause despair: "It confronted man with the alternatives of salvation and damnation, and filled him with the utmost anxiety for the fate of his soul."[6] In the Amherst of Emily Dickinson's time, personal experience of conversion was an event common to nearly all families.[7] Emily Dickinson early in life was seriously worried over being left out of "Christ's love" since she had never personally experienced any form of conversion. Her interest in death was an aspect of a continuing and profound concern over her own salvation.

Such apprehension is clearly evident in "Why should we hurry—why indeed" (III, 1646). It is almost as if, in her anxiety, she was urgently seeking to find some hint of her own salvation by examining death in all its forms. Questions of immortality came from all directions; any way she turned, she found herself "molested equally/ by immortality". The word *molested* is significant, implying that she was exceedingly troubled, almost pursued by the question of the post–mortem survival of her personality. Never able to forget its nearness, she allowed the question to color all of her thinking. She was never to find the assurance of salvation that she craved, and yet her awareness of the "bland uncertainty" of it all kept prodding her to continue in search of an answer —and kept her writing poetry.

Another poem distinctly expressive of Puritan concern over salvation is "A Pit—but Heaven over it—" (III, 1712). Heaven is all around, but also the Pit—and "To stir would be to slip—/ To look would be to drop". The poet must move with great circumspection and be wary even of dreams, for the wrong kinds could "sap the Prop/ That holds my chances up". Man is, indeed, in a precarious position; as Jonathan Edwards had so often reminded New Englanders, one and all are "sinners" subject to God's wrath.

And again, in a two–line fragment the poet writes, "is Immortality a bane/ That men are so oppressed?" (III,1728). Here clearly is a question expressing wonder, an implied request to be relieved from the necessity of having always to be alert to her prospects for salvation.

As early as 1891 William Dean Howells recognized Emily Dickinson's relation to Puritanism.

> There is no hint of what turned her life in upon itself, and probably this was its natural evolution, or involution, from tendencies inherent in the New England, or the Puritan, spirit.[8]

In discussing one of her poems he again pointed to the influence of her Puritan heritage:

> All that Puritan longing for sincerity, for veracious conduct, which in some good New England women's natures is almost a hysterical shriek, makes its exultant grim assertion in these lines.[9]

The Puritan preoccupation with religion, the emphasis on self–examination and renunciation, the anxiety created by desires for salvation—all were involved when, probably sometime in 1854, Emily came to a full realization that she could never formally join a church. Now she must face death without the consolations of the available orthodoxies.[10] This reaction was typical of Puritan behavior. Perry notes the importance, for the Puritan, of distrust of natural faculties, the importance of dependence on God and renunciation:

> They furnished the content of his meditation, and the object of his devotion on all the solemn occasions of his life—above all, when facing the prospect of death.[11]

In August, 1870, Emily Dickinson told T. W. Higginson that her father was the chief figure in her life.[12] Higginson came to believe that her father was from "*la vieille roche* of Puritanism", reading on Sunday "lonely

and rigorous books", and that he inspired her with awe
from childhood. Of the father, Higginson wrote that

> . . . it needed only a glance at his photograph to see
> how truly the Puritan tradition was preserved in him.
> He did not wish his children, when little, to read any-
> thing but the Bible.[13]

Emily's father, perhaps the most important single person in her life, was to her the living embodiment of the
Puritan tradition into which she had been born; his
mere existence made her unregenerate state seem the
more obvious by comparison. Edward Dickinson was
not a cruel or unkind man, but he was demanding of
himself and he expected his family to follow this example. He was a deeply religious man, devoted to his
family, but also active in civic and public affairs. He was
a successful lawyer, the treasurer of Amherst College for
thirty–eight years, several times a member of the state
legislature, and at one time served in Congress.[14]

Millicent Todd Bingham, whose mother was a neighbor of the Dickinsons and who, together with T. W.
Higginson, was the first editor of Emily Dickinson's
poems, believed that Emily was "governed in all respects
by her father's wishes".[15] She felt that while he was out-
spoken and frank in business affairs, he showed very
little affection and warmth within the family circle. He
demanded a smooth–running household and would excuse no carelessness in its management. He apparently
received complete obedience from every member of his
family—at least to the extent that none of them ever left

home. When his son took a wife, a home was provided for the newlyweds next door—and they lived in it, obediently. The elder Dickinson seems to have had strong convictions about everything in which he was personally involved—and much else, besides. It is rather typical that he was steadfast in support of the temperance movement:

> He not only believed in it; he considered its observance of practical importance, since failure to keep the pledge of total abstinence was a form of backsliding easily observed.[16]

Emily's letters reveal Edward Dickinson's influence on her. Fully aware that his wishes were important, she apparently did her best to please him. She wrote in 1850:

> I have always neglected the culinary arts, but attend to them now from necessity, and from a desire to make everything pleasant for father, and Austin.   (I, 97)

And in a letter dating from 1858 we find:

> I do not go out at all, lest father will come and miss me, or miss some little act, which I might forget, should I run away.   (II, 337)

Whether she was using her father as an excuse cannot be known, of course, but even if she were, the very fact that she would consider such an "excuse" plausible is significant.

It was typical of the man that Edward Dickinson should strongly disapprove of certain "modern" writers

and feel called upon to censor his daughter's reading.
She remarked to Austin, in a letter dating from 1853:

> Father was very severe to me; he thought I'd been
> trifling with you, so he gave me quite a trimming
> about "Uncle Tom" and "Charles Dickens" and these
> "modern Literati" who he says are *nothing*, compared
> to past generations, who flourished when *he was a boy*.
>
> (I, 237)

Nothing is gained by dwelling further on Edward
Dickinson's sternness, or on Emily's reaction to it. She
was evidently able, at times, to see something pompous
and slightly ludicrous in him. She described her father
on the opening day of the railroad between Palmer and
Amherst: "Father was, as usual, Chief Marshall of the
day, and went marching around the town with New
London at his heels like some old Roman General, upon
a Triumph Day" (I, 254).

In 1851 Jenny Lind gave a performance in Northampton, with the Dickinsons in the audience. Edward
Dickinson enjoyed her singing despite himself; his
daughter seems to have been as much interested in the
reaction of her father as in the performance of the
"Swedish Nightingale":

> Father sat all the evening looking *mad*, and *silly*, and
> yet so much amused you would have *died* a laughing.
> . . . It wasn't *sarcasm* exactly, nor it was'nt *disdain*, it
> was infinitely funnier than either of those virtues, as
> if old Abraham had come to see the show, and thought
> it was all very well, but a little excess of *Monkey*!
>
> (I, 121)

But while Emily could, under certain conditions, see the "Monkey" in her usually proper father, there is no question that he indeed "inspired her with awe from early childhood". When he died in Boston in June, 1874, her world was shaken, and she wrote to her cousins: "I thought I was strongly built, but this stronger has undermined me" (II, 526). In the same letter she told of how Austin came in with a dispatch, and she could see by his face that they were "all lost". The word *lost* indicates how strongly Emily had depended on her father. More than a year later, in a letter written in the summer of 1875, she spoke of "those amazing years that I had a father" (II, 543).

Actually the protectiveness that Edward Dickinson exerted did provide certain advantages for his daughter. It gave her a place to run to, a support to lean on. Yet at the same time, feeling as she did about religion, there was great tension created by his overwhelming presence. He preached a stern morality based on his Puritan past and was to his daughter the living symbol of a tradition to which she was drawn, yet against which she rebelled. Edward Dickinson *was* Puritanism to Emily, and her feelings about him were like her attitudes toward her Puritan heritage and the orthodox religion of her time. Far more than "awe" was involved. Her feelings covered a wide range of other emotions: fear, revolt, love, respect, ridicule.

It was Edward Dickinson, above all, who made Emily Dickinson aware of her Puritan past—who by his character and through his daily reading aloud from the

Bible made living a religious life seem not merely important, but all–important. Death, for the Puritan, was in a sense the apex of a life, the culminating point of a career, the most important and solemn of all occasions; for shortly one would discover whether he was to be saved as a member of the elect or to be rejected and left out of God's love. Edward Dickinson not only instilled in his daughter traditions from the past, but was the living reminder of the Puritan teachings. His presence served to aggravate her anxiety and apprehension over the prospect of death and what might await the soul of the departed. Edward Dickinson and his father before him had been intimately associated with the affairs of Amherst College. Millicent Todd Bingham reminds us that the Articles of Faith for the Church of Amherst College, as formulated in 1826, declared that:

> . . . all who die without repentance, will at the day of judgment be condemned for their own sins, and will remain in impenitence and justly suffer everlasting punishment.[17]

These words were not written by Edward Dickinson, but they accurately convey his convictions.

For one year, 1847-1848, Emily attended Mount Holyoke Seminary in South Hadley, Massachusetts, about ten miles from Amherst. Mary Lyon, founder of the institution, was devoted to the cause of education for women, and apparently maintained rather high academic standards. She had an equal concern, however, for the "spiritual welfare" of her charges, and the seminary was founded in the hope of spreading orthodox Congregationalist views. From a religious viewpoint the year was a crucial one for Emily Dickinson.[18]

Judged by twentieth-century standards, the atmosphere at Mount Holyoke may well seem grim and oppressive, but as George Frisbie Whicher has pointed out, Mount Holyoke was not an institution devoted to repressing and curbing all the natural instincts of youth.[19] Time was allowed for recreation, for entertaining male callers from Amherst College and elsewhere, and even for an occasional buggy ride with the young gentlemen. Mount Holyoke was in no sense a prison, and it would be untrue to suggest that Emily Dickinson's "free spirit" revolted against the Puritan "repression" of her college environment.

On the other hand, it is also true that the teachers and the founder of Mount Holyoke were deeply concerned with the religious life of their students, and time was set aside for special meetings where the impenitent might be given ample opportunity to experience "hope" and possible salvation.[20] It would be misleading to deny this side of Emily Dickinson's Mount Holyoke experience and the effect which this experience must have had on her own religious outlook. The now familiar story of Emily's inability to realize conversion has been expertly presented by Whicher in *This Was a Poet*, through the use of letters and certain passages from Mount Holyoke journals.

The strong pressure exerted on students at Mount Holyoke to "accept" Christ left its mark on Emily Dickinson. Her sense of religious inadequacy must have been greatly intensified as she witnessed the "conversion" of most of her classmates. The effect must have been doubly painful since she had looked forward with such pleasure to attending the school. There is no sign, judging from her letters, that she wanted to be a "rebel", or to be "different" merely for the sake of being so. On the contrary, there is ample evidence to indicate that she wanted to conform, wanted to accept religion in the manner of her contemporaries, but was honestly unable to do so. She did not experience any sort of personal conversion, and for her "pretending" was out of the question.

Her Mount Holyoke experience vividly impressed (and reimpressed) upon her the importance of salvation —and just as vividly reminded her of the fact that she had not personally felt any such "call" to Christ, and seemingly would never be able to do so. The prospect of dying without salvation undoubtedly deepened her apprehensions about death itself. Emily's year at Mount Holyoke, then, served to increase her anxious concern with death and to accentuate the tensions that are so markedly revealed in her poems on the subject.

Emily Dickinson was exposed, at least, to some of the writings of Margaret Fuller and Theodore Parker,[21] and she was quite familiar with the essays and poems of Ralph Waldo Emerson.[22] Emerson lectured in Amherst on several occasions during Emily Dickinson's lifetime, and though there is no positive evidence that she ever heard or met him, it is known that her brother and his wife entertained Emerson in their home.[23] Be that as it may, it was primarily through Emerson that her mind was opened to Transcendentalism. Coming during and soon after her Mount Holyoke ordeal, exposure to Transcendentalist thought acted, for the moment, to bolster her shaken ego.

However much or little Emily may have known about the Transcendentalists previously, it was principally through the influence of a young man named Benjamin F. Newton that she was exposed to their "radical" ideas impressively. Newton came to Amherst in the winter of 1847–1848 (while Emily was at Mount Holyoke) to study law in the office of Edward Dickinson. When he left Amherst in 1850, Newton was one of Emily's closest friends, and he continued to be until his death in 1853. To appreciate fully the significance of his awakening her mind to the "radical" literature of Transcendentalism and in particular to the writings of Emerson, it is necessary to remember that at this time Emerson was still feared by orthodox New Englanders as a dangerous liberal.[24]

Emily Dickinson was attracted to certain ideas in Transcendentalism as a reaction against the darker side of Puritanism.[25] Puritan thought and Transcendental thought were not, of course, in total opposition. Both were primarily concerned with spiritual and ethical values, both were concerned with the redemption of souls, both stressed aspiration to perfection in some sense of the term. At the risk of oversimplification, however, it is also possible to discern fundamental differences as to how these desiderata should be obtained.

Transcendentalism asserted that all men were per-
fectible in this life. Puritanism conceded that perfection was possible, but only to some men, and even for
these not in this life. Transcendentalism emphasized the
self–sufficiency of the individual; Puritanism, his dependency. Puritanism's emphasis on humility and acknowledgment of man's undeservingness ran counter
to Emerson's belief in the sufficiency of the private man.
Dependence as opposed to self–reliance, the helpless-
ness of the natural man as opposed to the divinity of
the natural man, the insistence on duty as opposed to
spontaneity, trust in traditional authority as opposed
to the individual's trust in his own vision, the moral
dependence of the individual as opposed to his moral
finality—these are the contrasts that probably appealed
to Emily Dickinson. Such contrasts no doubt are only
partial truths, but this darker side of Puritanism did
exist, and because of her unhappy experience at Mount
Holyoke, this side was probably uppermost in Emily's
thoughts, and perhaps seemed all the darker beside the
optimism of Transcendentalism.

Emerson preached confidence in man's inner sense
of worth.[26] After Emily's failure to accept religion in the
orthodox manner of her contemporaries at Mount Holyoke and the profound disturbance it caused in her own
mind, the writings of Emerson must have given her new
hope and renewed confidence. Faith in the potentialities of man, as conveyed by Emerson's words, must have
been soothing to one who recently had been reminded

that she was not one of the "elect". Emerson wrote in *Nature*:

> Who can set bounds to the possibilities of man? Once inhale the upper air, being admitted to behold the absolute natures of justice and truth, and we learn that man has access to the entire mind of the Creator, is himself the creator in the finite.

A similar thought appears in "The American Scholar". The one thing of value is the "active Soul", and this "every man is entitled to; this every man contains within him". Perfectibility is possible for all, here and now, and is not restricted to a select few; no one is "out of grace". Again, in "Self Reliance" he spoke of "that divine idea which each of us represents". In "Compensation" he wrote that "The soul refuses limits, and always affirms an Optimism, never a Pessimism".

Particularly gratifying to Emily must have been "The Divinity School Address" on how the churches had failed in their duty to teach "the soul". Emerson could see the Church losing control of the people: "The Church seems to totter to its fall, almost all life extinct". Later in the same address he said that "It is already beginning to indicate character and religion to withdraw from the religious meetings". To one who felt left out of the orthodox religion of her time, and who was soon to stop going to church, Emerson's words must have been reassuring indeed.

It is easy to find echoes of some of these thoughts in Emily Dickinson's poems. The idea of the self–sufficiency of each individual she expresses in, "Obtaining

but our own Extent/ In whatsoever Realm" (III, 1543).
Even Christ illustrates the principle of the "active
soul": " 'Twas Christ's own personal Expanse/ That
bore him from the Tomb". The sense of inner worth
and self–reliance she writes of in, "Never for Society/
He shall seek in vain—/ Who His own acquaintance/
Cultivate" (II, 746). Each individual must follow his
own vision, must independently achieve his own
growth; and no outside authority is needed: "Growth
of man—like Growth of Nature—/ Gravitates within"
(II, 750); and Man himself, not an external agency,
must achieve the goal: "Each—it's difficult Ideal/ Must
achieve—Itself".

Emerson wrote in "Compensation":

> Polarity, or action and reaction, we meet in every
> part of nature; in darkness and light; in heat and cold;
> in the ebb and flow of waters; in male and female; in
> the inspiration and expiration of plants and animals.

This same pull of opposites can be seen in the nature
of man: "Every excess causes a defect; every defect an
excess. Every sweet hath its sour; every evil its good".
Emily Dickinson could write, "Good, without alarm/
Is a too established Fortune—/ Danger—Deepens Sum"
(II, 807). There is no mistaking the idea in "Water, is
taught by thirst./ Land—by the Oceans passed./ Transport—by throe—/ Peace—by it's battles told" (I, 135). A
total lack of contrast would not be desirable, for then
"The Value could not be—/ We buy with contrast—
Pang is good/ As near as memory" (II, 1133).

Did she find, through a complete acceptance of Transcendentalism, a release from her Puritan roots? The answer, of course, is that she did not. Firmly embedded in her character, her Puritan past could not be completely sloughed off. Puritan ideas, as well as Transcendentalist ones, continued to make their influence felt in her writings.

The ultimate result of her exposure to Emersonian Transcendentalism was somewhat curious. The immediate effect was to give her spirits a needed lift, to make her more aware of aspects of human nature other than the ones emphasized at Mount Holyoke. The end effect, however, was almost the reverse: Emily Dickinson could not fully endorse the ideas of either Puritanism or Transcendentalism, and since she found both unsatisfying, each served to highlight the other. Thus abstract philosophy—whether in the form of Puritanism or Transcendentalism—gave her no satisfactory explanation of man's place in the universe. And it was the lack in these "systems"—a lack made especially vivid through opposition—that turned her in the direction of existentialism. Man's ultimate role, she perhaps felt, was not a problem for "thought" at all, but could be considered only through the "solitary experience" of poetry. The optimistic affirmations of man's hopes and potentialities made just that much more vivid the Puritan's pessimistic awareness of man's precarious position. An added tension was thus created, and this increased anxiety was brought to a focus when her mind dwelt on death. The conflict set up between what she felt were two opposite views of man's nature served to add inten-

persons ranging in age from thirteen to thirty–three; in 1852, four, from ages eight to twenty–four; 1853, twelve, from ages eleven to thirty–two; and 1854, six, from ages seventeen to thirty–one.[30]

Little wonder, then, that one finds frequent references to death and illness in Emily Dickinson's letters. Her earliest firsthand knowledge of death came when she was thirteen, and the impression made was extremely distinct.[31] Two years following the actual incident she wrote of the experience to her friend, Abiah Root:

> My friend was Sophia Holland. . . . I visited her often in sickness & watched over her bed. But at length Reason fled and the physician forbid any but the nurse to go into her room. . . . At length the doctor said she must die & allowed me to look at her a moment through the open door. I took off my shoes and stole softly to the sick room.
>
> There she lay mild & beautiful . . . & her pale features lit up with an unearthly smile. I looked as long as friends would permit. . . . I shed no tear . . . but after she was laid in her coffin . . . I gave way to a fixed melancholy. (I, 32)

She closed her letter by saying that shortly afterward she went to Boston, where her health and spirits improved. This intense curiosity over physical aspects of death was to increase as she grew older.

Mrs. Bingham was highly alert to these more-than-occasional allusions to sickness and disease. In the next several paragraphs I rely on some of her observations.

Frequent references to illness and death in Emily Dickinson's letters appear almost casual, as if they were so much a part of her life as to be rather commonplace. This does not mean that she ever became calloused toward death or illness, for she continued to show extreme concern and sympathy for families experiencing such troubles. But some of her early letters, written to close friends and relatives, show how such things were accepted as not uncommon facts in her life. In 1850 she mentioned to her friend Abiah that her mother, who apparently was never very strong, was again ill: "Everything has been done, and tho' we think her gradually throwing it off, she still has much suffering" (I, 97). In a letter to Austin, written in 1852, she somewhat facetiously commented on the difficult position of patients who must choose among evils in the various "schools" of medicine:

> "Mrs. Skeeter" is very feeble, "cant bear Allopathic treatment, cant have Homeopathic"—dont want Hydropathic—Oh what a pickle she is in—should'nt think she would deign to *live*—it is so decidedly vulgar!
> (I, 190–91)

To a friend, in 1846, she wrote of having just seen a funeral procession: "I have just seen a funeral procession go by of a negro baby, so if my ideas are rather dark you need not marvel" (I, 24).

A letter to Mrs. J. G. Holland written in 1866 simply and directly mentions the death of a neighbor: "A woman died last week, young and in hope but a little

while—at the end of our garden" (II, 453). An 1851 letter to Austin, in which she wrote that their sister Lavinia had "reserved the *deaths* for me", since "*she* has
detailed the *news*" (I, 138), indicates just how frequent
and to–be–expected was news of death—so common, in
fact, that it was not even considered news.[32]

When Emily lived on Pleasant Street, from 1840 to
1855, the Dickinson home was close by the village
cemetery.[33] The fact that nearly all the funeral proces-
sions passed Emily Dickinson's house would almost
force upon her the frequent consciousness of death and
also give her ample opportunity of studying at firsthand
the ceremonies and trappings connected with funerals.

The source of many of her poems treating the physical aspects of death was firsthand experience. Her observation of funerals and burials, the familiar experience
of the death of friends and neighbors, the vivid impressions made upon her in the presence of the dying—
these furnished the basis for many of the concrete
images in her death poems. Puritanism and Transcendentalism provided the material for abstract
thoughts and concepts connected with death and immortality; but first–person observation of certain facts
and physical aspects of death provided concrete, em-
pirical evidence. At times, the observable facts of physical death seemed to offer little support for certain
concepts of immortality or eternity. At other times,
physical death did seem to impress her as a mere stage,
an entry to something beyond this life. In her better
poems, whatever the thoughts are, their power is based

largely on her ability to express the thoughts in concrete terms—and the source for many of these concrete terms was firsthand experience.

Although Emily Dickinson was no "Civil War Poet" in the ordinary sense, it is more than mere coincidence that the Civil War years were also those of her greatest creative productivity—at least in terms of the number of poems written. Thomas H. Johnson gives tentative dates to 1,656 of her 1,775 known poems. Of the 1,656, more than half—852—were composed between 1861 and 1865. To determine whether more than coincidence is involved, one must consider how the war affected Amherst and the Dickinsons and, more specifically, how Emily felt about it. Mrs. Bingham in *Emily Dickinson's Home* points to significant letters, and I follow her lead.

The war certainly does not figure in her poetry as it does, for example, in Whitman's or Melville's, but it did bring about in her a heightened awareness of death. Prior to the war, there were a few southern students in Amherst College, and these left the town when the war began. Apparently the school and the town responded to the request for enlistments, and it was not long before loss was felt by Amherst. A neighbor of the Dickinsons lost two sons early in the conflict, and Emily wrote of the fact to her cousin:

> Mrs. Adams had news of the death of her boy to-day, from a wound at Annapolis. Telegram signed by Frazer Stearns. You remember him. Another one died in October—from fever caught in the camp. Mrs. Adams

herself has not risen from bed since then. "Happy new year" step softly over such door as these! . . . Poor little widow's boy, riding to-night in the mad wind, back to the village burying-ground where he never dreamed of sleeping! (II, 386)

The Frazer Stearns mentioned in the letter was the son of the president of Amherst College and was apparently quite friendly with the Dickinsons. Emily seems to have somehow anticipated his death, or at least the possibility of it, for in the same letter she wrote: "Frazer Stearns is just leaving Annapolis. His father has gone to see him to–day. I hope that ruddy face won't be brought home frozen" (II, 386).

Her intuition was right, for in March, 1862, Frazer Stearns was killed in action at Newbern and his body brought to Amherst for burial. The death of a close acquaintance thus gave her an intimate realization of war. The effect can be seen in a letter written to her Norcross cousins, in which she told of Stearns' bravery, expressed her own deep sorrow over his death, and then characteristically described certain details connected with transporting the body and with the funeral in Amherst:

Just as he fell, in his soldier's cap, with his sword at his side, Frazer rode through Amherst. Classmates . . . to guard his narrow face! He fell by the side of Professor Clark, his superior officer. . . . Sanderson, his classmate, made a box of boards in the night, put the brave boy in, covered with a blanket, rowed six miles to reach the boat—so poor Frazer came. . . . Nobody here could

look on Frazer—not even his Father. The doctors would
not allow it.

The bed on which he came was enclosed in a large
casket shut entirely, and covered from head to foot
with the sweetest flowers. He went to sleep from the
village church. Crowds came to tell him good-night,
choirs sang to him, pastors told how brave he was—
early-soldier heart.   (II, 397–98)

There is evidenced here, again, an almost clinical
interest in physical details of death and its aftermath.[34]
Especially interesting is a letter written considerably
later in the war, probably in 1864:

Sorrow seems more general than it did, and not the
estate of a few persons, since the war began; and if the
anguish of others helped one with one's own, now
would be many medicines.   (II, 436)

Certain inferences may be drawn here. First, the war
served to increase her awareness of death. A great many
people were involved in the business of killing; death
was a very real presence; and even those far from the
battlefield could not help taking notice of war's horrid
effects. Second, the war made her all the more vividly
aware of the universality of death—of the fact that it
was not "the estate of a few persons". *All* must face
death themselves, and *all* must be influenced by the
impact of death on those still living.

To her cousins she commented that she was at first
astonished when she learned that Robert Browning had
"made another poem", astonished that he could write

anything more after the death of his wife in 1861—
astonished, that is, "till I remembered that I, myself,
in my smaller way, sang off charnel steps. Every day
life feels mightier, and what we have the power to be,
more stupendous" (II, 436). She "sang off charnel
steps". Here is a clear implication that death was a
great stimulus to her writing, lending support to the
belief that the Civil War served to rouse her creative
energy. At the same time, the war, as a symbol of death,
emphasized the value of life—its rarity and "might",
the fact that it could be cut short serving to increase
her eagerness to create. Herein lay the reason behind
the statement, "Every day life feels mightier, and what
we have the power to be, more stupendous".

Already highly sensitive to death, Emily Dickinson
responded to the war with heightened creative activity.
She did not respond, as did Whitman, with a series of
so–called Civil War poems—no "Drum-Taps", no
"Memories of President Lincoln"—but she did write
at least four poems directly inspired by the Civil War.
Far more significantly, however, as a result of the war
she intensified her efforts to understand death, poetically testing her ideas in the increased creative output
of these years.

General Characteristics
of
Emily Dickinson's Poetry

❖

EARLY IN LIFE EMILY DICKINSON FOUND
a verse form that suited her. She wrote practically no
free verse, using rhyme and meter in the overwhelming
majority of her poems. Contrary to some popular opinion, she did not make many radical innovations in verse
form. Basically, she used meters derived from the hymn
books to which she was exposed as a child in church
and at home. Her father owned a copy of Isaac Watts'
Christian Psalmody in which the meter for each song
was named. Watts' book also had an introduction in
which various meters and their suitability for particular occasions were treated. Whicher and Johnson
have both described in detail how the hymn meters
were the source of her verse form.[1]

There were three major iambic meters. The "common meter" consisted of four–line stanzas, alternately
four and three feet to a line, similar to ballad meter.
The "long meter" differed from the "common" in that

all lines had four feet. "Short meter" had two lines of three feet, then one line of four, then the final line back to three. There were also traditionally accepted arrangements for trochaic and dactyllic meters. Emily Dickinson wrote the majority of her poems in "common meter", though she did use practically all of the principal meters of the hymn books.[2]

She did go, however, beyond her models. In order to avoid the rather monotonous and mechanical regularity of the hymns, she introduced variations within accepted patterns. She substituted an occasional trochaic foot in place of the expected iambic, introduced an extra final syllable, or dropped a final syllable. On occasion, she used several different types of meter in the same poem.

From the outset, almost by accident, Emily Dickinson found the verse pattern which, with variations, she was to continue to use throughout the years. Fortunately relieved from a need to be overly concerned about external form, she was able to focus her creative attention on what she had to say. At the same time, her freedom within this form did not make her force meaning to fit some completely rigid and inflexible metrical pattern.

Emily Dickinson's frequent use of approximate rhyme has attracted widespread attention, and early critics, such as Thomas Bailey Aldrich, objected vigorously to it. Even her first editors, Mrs. Todd and T. W. Higginson, felt that her use of false rhyme might prejudice the public against her verse, and in some cases

they altered words to effect a rhyme. Her irregularities
in rhyme did defy the common practice of her day, but
there was a possible precedent for them in poems by
Ralph Waldo Emerson.

Emerson occasionally used what is sometimes called
suspended rhyme—that is, different vowel sounds followed by identical consonants. In "Each and All", for
example, he rhymes *Napoleon-noon, Wreath-breath*;
in "the Problem", *cowl-soul, sphere-air, shrine-within,
Ghost-lost*; in "The Humble-Bee", *waste–passed*. Perhaps a degree of caution is necessary in labeling all of
these rhymes irregular. Linguistic evidence might
show, at least occasionally, that these combinations
were "right" to Emerson's ear. It is safe to assume, however, that some of them were irregular, if not all.

It is hard to believe that Emily Dickinson did not
know how to make perfect rhyme! She had plenty of
examples before her in the hymn books. She had read
Longfellow, Poe, Lowell, Holmes. Her correspondence
with Higginson had made it clear to both that her
rhymes were not exact, and he would have been de-
lighted to instruct her in the art of making true rhymes.
One must conclude, therefore, that she made use of
approximate rhyme intentionally.[3] Answering Higginson, who once suggested that she give up rhyme alto-
gether, she replied that she "could not drop the Bells
whose jingling cooled my Tramp" (II, 408). Apparently, she wanted the musical effect of rhyme, but did not
wish to restrict herself to exact rhyme. Just as she varied
the traditional hymn meters, she varied the traditional

rhyme. Her use of both exact and approximate rhyme gave her more freedom in her selection of words. It must be admitted that her irregularities were not always more effective than exact rhyme would have been; and perhaps many were more the result of haste than design. But she *did* choose to use approximate rhyme, and this choice *did* allow for greater range and freedom.

Another general characteristic of her verse—its compactness and concision—has received wide attention, as have her idiosyncrasies in grammar and syntax. Actually, the two are related. The fondness for condensation led her, at times, to omit articles, prepositions, conjunctions, auxiliary verbs. Such omissions, and her fondness for the subjunctive, account for most of Emily Dickinson's so–called evasions of rules of grammar.[4]

But the question arises: do these deviations from regularity in form "mean" anything? Is there evidence of any relationship between her subject matter and her form? More specifically, can any of her "irregularities" bear some relationship to her attitude toward death? The answer is—yes, some such relationship can be discerned.

Emily Dickinson's anxiety and concern over death and immortality, motivated by her religious doubts and insecurities, led her to recognize the presence of evil in the world. What *is* often conflicts with what *ought to be*! As she wrote Louise Norcross: "wholes are not below" (III, 671). The universe is not intact; there is a lack of harmony, and the world is fragmented. Is it possible that she tried to picture the disordered

nature of the universe through irregularities in rhyme
and meter? Is it possible that she used exact rhyme only
in those poems in which a positive conviction was expressed, or only in "light" verse in which death and
evil were not primary concerns? Did she use approximate rhyme and irregular meter only in poems in which
she expressed her doubts and her view that the universe
was fragmented, or only in those poems concerned with
death? Such relationships would constitute a very neat
pattern, indeed, if it existed. Unfortunately, it does
not.[5] In an early poem mourning the death of a girl,
expressing sorrow over her departure, one might expect
to find irregular rhyme and irregular meter. But in the
first stanza—

> She went as quiet as the Dew
> From an Accustomed flower.
> Not like the Dew, did she return
> At the Accustomed hour!   (I, 149)

the rhyme is exact, and the meter is the exactly regular
"common meter" of the hymn books. Another poem,
somewhat later, expresses profound disillusion. Here, if
ever, one might expect to find irregularities. The poet
was disappointed in an idol—

> Yet blamed the Fate that fractured—*less*
> Than I reviled Myself,
> For entertaining Plated Wares
> Upon my Silver Shelf—   (II, 747)

Again the rhyme is exact, and the meter is once more
the "common meter". But in the rhyme and meter of
a typical "light" poem, about winter—

> These are the days that Reindeer love
> And pranks the Northern star
> This is the Sun's objective
> And Finland of the Year   (III, 1696)

she uses suspended rhyme and a combination of meters —dactylic, trochaic, and iambic. As a final example, consider this "light" poem about a parasol:

> The parasol is the umbrella's daughter,
> And associates with a fan
> While her father abuts the tempest
> And abridges the rain.   (III, 1747)

Here she uses suspended rhyme and a mixture of anapest and iambic feet, and no two lines have the same number of syllables.

The fact that there is no convenient one-to-one relationship between form and substance does not mean there is no relationship at all. Indeed, that her poetry did not conform to the pattern considered above suggests what this relationship is. For Emily Dickinson to have followed the pattern would have been inconsistent with her belief that "wholes are not below". She did not picture the world in terms of simple dichotomies. It was not a case of either–or. Things were not all good or all evil, all harmony or all discord, all regular meter or all irregular meter, all true rhyme or all false rhyme. The universe was a mixture of good and evil, black and white, exact rhyme and approximate rhyme. She chose to convey this insight by making her verse a mixture of regularities and irregularities. The world was a mingling of harmony and disharmony, a complex and intri-

cate arrangement. Similarly, her verse is a combination
of assonance and rhyme, uniform hymn book meter and
deviations.

In 1955 the publication of the Harvard edition of
her poems made it possible to view the whole range of
her work. As long as one is aware that the dating of the
poems is approximate—handwriting analysis is not an
exact science—it is possible to discern the main lines in
her development, and to suggest the following tentative
arrangement. Emily Dickinson's poems seem to fall
into three distinct periods, the works in each period
having certain general characteristics in common.[6]
Poems written before 1861 comprise the first group;
those from 1861–1865, the second; and those from 1866
and after, the third. In assigning approximate dates to
the poems, Johnson offers the following breakdown:
Before 1861, she composed a total of 215 poems, all but
five of which date from between 1858 and 1861. Between 1861 and 1865, she composed 852; and from
1866 to 1886, the year of her death, she composed 589.[7]

There is, of course, a certain overlapping of characteristics from one period to another, and it is not
possible to identify individual poems by characteristics
alone as belonging to a particular period. Read as a
group, however, the poems in each period possess
certain general qualities in common. The poetry before
1861, by comparison with that which she wrote later
in life, is somewhat conventional and sentimental. The
gift–books, magazines, and newspapers of the mid-
nineteenth century gave death, in the form of "funereal

poetry", particular emphasis. It was the effusive senti-
ment displayed by this kind of poetry that led Mark
Twain to satirize this fad by creating the figure of
Emmeline Grangerford in *Huckleberry Finn*. While
Emily Dickinson's early poetry, in relation to that
written later, is somewhat sentimental, it rarely approaches the exaggerated emotion of the popular
funereal verse. It was no little triumph for Emily Dickinson that she succeeded in transcending the prevalent
maudlin sentimentality.[8]

And yet her poetry before 1861 is lacking in the
intensity and sense of urgency that is so characteristic
of her later work, and especially of the poems in the
middle period. There is not the strong overtone of the
anguish she felt in being one of the "unregenerate".
The tension is not yet present in her verse. There is
little of that condensation and syntactical shorthand,
effected largely through the omission of auxiliary verbs
and the omission of pronouns, that is found in her later
verse. The early poetry is really more of a "reflection"
in verse than it is a presentation of ideas through combinations of concrete images. The period before 1861
was her apprenticeship, spent in learning how to write
poetry, in building her confidence and skill in the use
of words through actual writing. Understandably, these
poems are not her best. Though it was in this early
period that she discovered the basic ideas that she was
to continue to use in her study of death, she had not yet
perfected her technique.

The time between 1861 and 1865 was Emily Dickinson's most creative period, and during these years her talent reached maturity. These characteristics reached full development: the sense of tension and urgency; the joining of the like with the unlike; the combination of abstract speculation on death and immortality with observed fact; the use of homely terms to express Puritan doubts or Transcendental hopes, or to express her own dilemma created by the opposite pull of these two poles. Her religious predicament was critical during this period, and the Civil War plus the removal of her "spiritual preceptor", the Reverend Charles Wadsworth, intensified her religious doubts. The poetry of this time reflects her anxiety.

Whereas the poems from 1861 to 1865 are quite frequently a vigorous, and yet not bitter or despairing, protest against the inscrutability of death, those written later are more pessimistic. The poetry continues to question the purpose of death, and continues to express hope for immortality, but there is a tendency in her later poems to dwell more on the apparent hopelessness of solving the "riddle" in this life. As the years passed, she became increasingly more resentful of the anxiety caused by her religious doubts. She wrote some of her finest poetry during this period, but the intensity and the insistency characteristic of the period from 1861 to 1865 gradually diminished, giving way to a somewhat pessimistic and at times slightly cynical resentment.

Awareness of these general characteristics—a blending of regularities and irregularities—and recognition of the particular qualities belonging to each of the three periods now put the reader in a position to consider the poems in some detail. As Charles Anderson writes:

> To give her poetry the serious attention it deserves is the real task that remains. To study it intensively, to stare a hole in the page until these apparently cryptic notations yield their full meanings—this is the great challenge to modern readers.[9]

IV

Apprenticeship

❖

IN CHAPTERS IV, V, AND VI, I WILL RE-
view in some detail Emily Dickinson's poems of death,
attempting to show how various approaches to death in
her poetry reflect her need to relieve religious stress
and anxiety, her need to view the many shapes of death.
Her poetic "technique" will also be examined. By
"technique" is meant not only external form, the
"envelope" into which she poured the content, but the
actual arrangement of words in the poem, the connotations of words within the context of the poem, and the
pressures exerted on one word by another.[1] The manner
in which she arranged her poetic experience into a
structure of words can be understood only by scrutiny
of individual poems. No easy formula will explain her
poetry.

The Harvard edition of the poems includes redac-
tions, variants, and alternative readings. Though Emily
Dickinson was apparently inconsistent in the way she

entered suggested changes in her manuscripts, this edition places all such alternative readings at the end of the poems. While most of her poems survive in single drafts only, variant readings and different versions do exist for a number of them, and the reader has access to these in the Harvard edition.

Among Emily Dickinson's early poems on death, four general types or categories are prominent: (1) poems dealing with death and immortality, (2) poems dealing mainly with the physical aspects of death, (3) poems that personify death, and (4) elegiac poems. Naturally there is some overlapping, but most of the poems fall naturally into one or another group. This classification is useful in treating the large number of poems on death, for it allows choice of examples illustrating each type. Since her later poems continue this grouping, these headings are a convenient tool in discussing the entire range of her poetry on this subject. In their studies, Whicher, Chase, and Johnson make out a somewhat similar pattern. Ruth F. McNaughton, writing in the *Prairie Schooner*, XXIII (Summer, 1949), 203–15, also recognizes a four–part grouping, but two of her groups differ significantly from those presented here. And in all of the classifications mentioned both the treatment of the particular groups and the selection of poems for analysis generally differ from what follows below.

A word of caution may be in order. To assume that the "I", the speaker, the voice of the poems, is Emily Dickinson would be a basic error. Her poems are artistic creations, not history or personal narrative. Emily Dickinson, as most creative artists, had several dramatic masks. The "persona" of the poems certainly is not autobiographical. To see in each poem a literal reflection or projection of personal experience would be a mistake. For the sake of convenience in analyzing the poems, however, I have sometimes taken the liberty of speaking of "she", or "Emily Dickinson", or "the poet", trusting that the reader will assume the distinction between the historical person and the "fictive I" of the poems on the occasions where no distinction is made.

Among the early poems the largest group is that dealing with death and immortality.[2] These are her more obviously religious poems, expressing the Puritan idea of this life as a test for the next, expressing her concern and fear that she will not be among the elect. The earliest poem concerned with death and immortality, beginning "The feet of people walking home / With gayer sandals go" (I, 7), she wrote about 1858. It consists of three stanzas of eight lines each, with lines two and four, and six and eight in each stanza having perfect rhyme. One popular arrangement in the hymn books was that of alternating seven and six syllables to the line, with an iambic meter, and this method is what she has employed here. The poem expresses a hope for immortality. Just as the crocus, after rising above the ground, is no longer the "Vassal of the snow", we can hope for a better life in the future. Even here, however, one senses a note of doubt. Observation gave the poet no assurance: "My figures fail to tell me/ How far the Village lies". The poem is important as an early illustration of the intimate relation she saw between death and immortality. Death is "but our rapt attention to Immortality". The importance of death, then, lies in its relation to immortality.

Another poem, dating probably from 1858, shows the contradiction between observed fact and a religious hope for immortality. Though the tension is not yet present in her verse, it is present in the idea. Sailors, observing a sinking boat, can say only that it is lost, but angels can say that it "Retrimmed it's masts—redecked it's sails—/ And shot—exultant on!" The poem is a good, or perhaps bad, example of just how sentimental and conventional some of her early verse could be:

> Adrift! A little boat adrift!
> And night is coming down!
> Will *no* one guide a little boat
> Unto the nearest town?   (I, 30)

The poem beginning "I hav'nt told my garden yet" (I, 50), which she also wrote probably in 1858, is an early example of that sense of mystery and doubt which she always associated with death. In many of Emily Dickinson's later poems there is a kind of dramatic tension between her fancies about death, untestable through observation, and a background of closely observed fact. Rarely in her early poetry did she achieve the effect by her choice of words, but the germ for the later development was there. This poem dwells on the knowledge that the "persona" is mortal and will die. It is as if death were an honor and an achievement. She is rather embarrassed to mention death to her garden, or the shops in the street, or the hillsides. "That one so shy—so ignorant/ Should have the face to die" seems almost an impertinence. One can see here the Puritan emphasis on the solemnity and importance of the occasion of death. What will happen after death? Only the dead know. One feels as if Emily Dickinson at times enjoyed this suspense and mystery of death and immortality. It was the absorbing problem of her life. What would death lead to? It was not *a* riddle, but *the* riddle. She must watch herself and not be heedless and "Hint that within the Riddle/ One will walk today".

A poem of 1859, "As Watchers hang upon the East" (I, 121), compares an imagined heaven to a satisfaction of certain senses. Heaven, as a concept of the mind, is tempting to us; just as one waits in anticipation for a beautiful sunrise (or as the wise men viewed the star in the East), as a beggar longing for a feast imagines its savoriness, as one thirsting in the desert hears a babbling brook, "Heaven beguiles the tired". When the sunrise is witnessed, when the beggar is the guest, when thirst is satisfied—these experiences must be what heaven is like. Yet the poem ends on a typical note of doubt. It will be "Heaven to us, if true". Characteristically, the poet came back to observed fact after a flight of fancy. This combination of fact and fancy gave to her verse a sense of conflict and tension. When she stopped merely stating this idea—that there is often a disparity between concepts of the mind and observed facts, between the way we would like things to be and the way things actually are; when she stopped merely stating this idea and let the images speak for themselves, her poetry reached its maturity.

Perhaps the rhyme in this poem deserves notice. In the first stanza lines one and two end in perfect rhyme, *east–feast*. The words *spread–tired*, ending lines three and six, and the words *sweet–delight*, ending lines four and five, form what is sometimes called suspended rhyme, that is, different vowel–sounds followed by identical consonants. In the second stanza, *east–amethyst* form a suspended rhyme, *go–true* a vowel rhyme, and *guest–pressed* a perfect rhyme, assuming that the *–ed* is aspirated and not voiced. This use of approximate rhyme became more frequent as she continued to write.

The idea of the struggling soul, the battle with one's own spirit in this world for reward in the next she expressed in a poem of 1859, beginning "To fight aloud is very brave" (I, 126). Again she stated the idea rather flatly, merely reflecting in verse, with none of the juxtaposition of abstract thought and concrete fact characteristic of her later verse. The inward struggle is more difficult than any external battle. Those struggling with their own souls may win, or fall, or die, and no one will have observed. This is the way things are; one who observes the facts would have no way of discovering this inward battle. Still, it is possible to hope for a heaven that will recognize the struggle and reward the one who makes it. Her Puritan background is again obvious. The last stanza reads:

We trust, in plumed procession
For such, the Angels go—
Rank after Rank, with even feet—
And Uniforms of Snow.

A poem from 1860 clearly expresses anxiety and concern over being accepted by heaven. It is the poem beginning " 'Tis so much joy! 'Tis so much joy!" (I, 172).
The "supposed person" has ventured all upon a single
throw and will prepare herself for heaven. Even if she
fails, "Defeat means nothing *but* Defeat", and death is
nothing but death. She is satisfied with her choice, even
if she has made the wrong one. What if she be right?
The single throw, then, will have been worth everything. The idea of winning the victory is so overwhelming to her that she almost fears being extinguished by
an actual heaven:

And if I gain! Oh Gun at Sea!
Oh Bells, that in the Steeples be!
At first, repeat it slow!
For Heaven is a different thing,
Conjectured, and waked sudden in—
And might extinguish me!

The subject was an extremely important one to Emily
Dickinson, just as it was to the Puritans, and her anxiety is clearly in evidence.

It appears that early in life Emily Dickinson accepted
the fact that she could not solve the riddle of death
while she was on this earth. Yet in spite of this realization, she could not refrain from observing death, hoping to find some clue in the appearance or in the last

words of the dying. Were they admitted to some secret at this time, withheld until this precise moment of dying?[3] Though she never gave up her investigation of the riddle, there is at times the indication that she wished she could end the quest. On occasion she became weary of being "molested" by death. In such a mood she could write, about 1860, that after all "I shall know why—when Time is over—/ And I have ceased to wonder why" (I, 193). The anguish generated by her pursuit of the "riddle" will be explained after death: "I shall forget the drop of Anguish/ That scalds me now—that scalds me now!"

There are other poems before 1861 which fall into the first group, but the ones presented give a fair sampling of this category. Her primary interest in death in these poems has been its intimate relation to immortality.

The second group treats the physical aspects of death.[4] Here, her major source was the observation of the dying, the dead, and the effects or aftermath of death as seen in burials, funerals, and household activities. These poems were based largely on her own intimate experience of the death of friends and neighbors in Amherst.

A poem from 1858 provides an early example of how she utilized the vivid impressions made upon her in the presence of the dying. The first stanza reads:

> There's something quieter than sleep
> Within this inner room!
> It wears a sprig upon it's breast—
> And will not tell it's name.   (I, 45)

Emily Dickinson here uses the very old comparison of sleep and death. There is a device present in this poem which she was to continue to use in showing the impersonality of the dead. Her observation of the radical change from life to death strongly impressed Emily Dickinson. One who only a moment ago had been a person suddenly became something that was not a person. To express this lack of personality she often used the neuter pronoun *it*. In this particular poem this pronoun (or its possessive) appears seven times in the first two stanzas. Remembering that this "something" was very recently a human being makes one more vividly aware of its present condition. The fact that it *wears* a sprig reminds one of its former human qualities. It once had a *name*, which it no longer will tell.

Thomas Johnson has observed how the utter silence of the dead deeply impressed Emily Dickinson.[5] Her sense of the lack of communication between the living and the dead, of their complete separateness, found frequent expression in her poetry. Her own existential "solitariness" was thus emphasized. The dead are the ones who could solve the "riddle", and their refusal to communicate is exasperating. This idea she presents by her use of *will*. She does not say *cannot* tell its name, but *will* not, as if through some perversity the dead "it" refuses to speak.

As Richard Chase observes, lack of motion was another attribute of the dead that vividly impressed Emily Dickinson.[6] Notice the second stanza:

> Some touch it, and some kiss it—
> Some chafe it's idle hand—
> It has a simple gravity
> I do not understand!

This utter stillness she chose to suggest by the adjective *idle*. The word conveys inactivity, but also overtones of resentment against the dead for being lazy or indolent, as if the dead had a choice in the matter and preferred to remain motionless. Coupled with her resentment against the dead is a sense of awe. It possesses a "simple gravity I do not understand".

The third stanza voices her objection to weeping over the dead. This still, silent, incomprehensible thing may well object, may even find it "rude in one to sob!" Yet such a presence, resting in "simple gravity", surely deserves some recognition or tribute. This is given, in the last stanza, not by weeping, but by indirection: "Birds have fled!" The dead may prefer this to a sob.

The poem is in "common meter", with a few truncated lines. She uses exact rhyme, suspended rhyme in *room–name*, and something that cannot be called either imperfect or suspended rhyme in *sob–wood*. Though neither the vowel nor the consonant sounds are identical, there is the barest echo of a rhyme. Her variations are working here, however mild. Even at this early stage, she was too much the creative artist to be rigidly bound by tradition.

A number of Emily Dickinson's early poems, not well imagined and having little intrinsic value, deserve men-

tion simply because they reflect her interest in cemeteries. The poem beginning "When Roses cease to
bloom, Sir" (I, 32), which she wrote in 1858, contains
the rather trite reflection that the hand which today
gathered flowers, someday "Will idle lie—in Auburn".
This reference is to Mt. Auburn Cemetery in Cambridge, which she had visited in August, 1846. She
wrote her friend Abiah from Boston:

> Have you ever been to Mount Auburn? If not you can
> form but slight conception of the "City of the dead."
> It seems as if Nature had formed the spot with a dis-
> tinct idea in view of its being a resting place for her
> children, where wearied & disappointed they might
> stretch themselves beneath the spreading cypress &
> close their eyes.   (I, 36)

The letter is effusively sentimental, as might be expected from a school girl of sixteen. The point is, however, that the cemetery vividly impressed her. There are
few allusions of any sort in Emily Dickinson's poetry,
and the fact that she mentioned Auburn by name shows
how deep the impression was.

Another such poem of 1858 exemplifies her interest
in graveyards. Here the cemetery is not a "city" but a
"village":

> I often passed the village
> When going home from school—
> And wondered what they did there—
> And why it was so still—   (I, 51)

The remainder of the poem includes the reflection that

the speaker will have an early death, and offers Austin Dickinson's wife, Sue, the "comforting" announcement that when the latter becomes tired, perplexed, or cold, her sister–in–law will be waiting in the grave to "enfold" her. It is not a well conceived poem, but one can imagine that Emily Dickinson indeed "often passed the village / When going home from school", since the Dickinson orchard adjoined the cemetery.

Another of her early musings inspired by cemeteries, which she wrote in 1859, expresses the idea that the grave is a comforter—certainly not an original thought and, in this particular poem, one not given an especially original treatment. But the verse does illustrate how her early poetry reflects her observations of cemeteries. The poem begins "Some, too fragile for winter winds / The thoughtful grave encloses" (I, 141). The grave is almost like a nurse or mother who "tenderly" tucks her children in. The grave is also safe, for it never exposes its treasures, and the schoolboy and the hunter dare not go there. The grave is democratic, for "This covert have all the children".

The meter of the poem shows some inventiveness; she varies the rigid pattern of the hymn books by using a combination of iambic, trochaic, and dactylic feet. The rhyme, too, shows deviation from the usual pattern. The final words in the last lines of each of the three stanzas form exact rhyme, and the second lines of the first two stanzas end in exact rhyme. She did employ occasional variation from hymn book meter and rhyme in her early poetry.

A poem of 1859, beginning "On such a night, or such a night,/ Would anybody care" (I, 146), is important for its use of a device which Emily Dickinson was to employ later with great effectiveness, namely, her habit of ironically contrasting the stillness and silence of the dead with the busy activity surrounding the care of a household. Though a minor part of the poem, its presence is unmistakable. The poem imagines a "little figure" too sound asleep,

> For Chanticleer to wake it—
> Or stirring house below—
> Or giddy bird in orchard—
> Or early task to do?

Thus *Chanticleer, stirring house, early task* all serve to heighten the reader's awareness of inactivity of the dead. The graveyard again makes its appearance: for every "knoll" or mound there was a "little figure plump", and for each child there were "Busy needles, and spools of thread". This last is a good example of Emily Dickinson's use of terms connected with her own household duties and activities—*busy needles, spools of thread*—in her poems of death. When she uses these in close association with some spiritual or religious conception of death, the effect can be startling.[7]

A poem of 1860, "Just lost, when I was saved!" (I, 160), is included in the present category for a particular reason. Though obviously not based on observed fact, the poem describes the imagined situation in terms of sensation. Emily Dickinson often thought in terms of

sensation, especially when composing her poems on the
physical aspects of death. The "persona" imagines that
she is on the verge of death, but then suddenly recovers:

> Just girt me for the onset with Eternity,
> When breath blew back,
> And on the other side
> I heard recede the disappointed tide!

The word *girt* is illustrative of the battle imagery
that Emily Dickinson so often used. The fictive "I"
is bracing herself to do battle with eternity, just as she
has struggled with her soul in this life. There will be a
clash, an onset with eternity. After the physical process
of life returned to her, after "breath blew back", she
heard death, in this case symbolized by tide, draw back.
In the second line of the poem she says that she *felt* the
world go by. Next time she knows there will be no
return and there will be things to see, and things "By
Ear unheard,/ Unscrutinized by Eye". The imagined
encounter with death and the hereafter is described in
terms of the senses.

One of the best realized of the early "poetic observations" on the physical aspects of death is "How many
times these low feet staggered" (I, 187), written about
1860. What were these observed facts in relation to the
dead? First of all, neither Puritanism nor Transcendentalism received any support from the silent, immobile thing under observation—more prosaically, the
corpse. Secondly, Emily Dickinson was impressed with
the complete incommunicability, immobility, and iso-

lation of the dead. Notice the first stanza of the poem:

> How many times these low feet staggered—
> Only the soldered mouth can tell—
> Try—can you stir the awful rivet—
> Try—can you lift the hasps of steel!

The poet wants a reply from the dead woman. Did she stagger under the burden of life? She is the only one who can answer, and her mouth is *soldered*. The frustration is acute. The *rivet* cannot be budged; the *hasps* are securely made of *steel*. Significantly, each of these four words is descriptive of some kind of metal. The dead one is like metal in several respects; she is as silent as metal and as firm in her refusal to reply. The observer will have as much difficulty getting an answer as he would in removing a rivet or opening a locked hasp of steel. Metal has a cold, hard surface, not unlike the appearance of the dead. There is further the idea of heaviness, weight, lack of motion associated with the two. Like a good metaphysical poet, Dickinson joins successfully objects which are ordinarily considered disparate.

She continues the metal image in the second stanza:

> Stroke the cool forehead—hot so often—
> Lift—if you care—the listless hair—
> Handle the adamantine fingers
> Never a thimble—more—shall wear.

Metal is ordinarily *cool* and usually requires *lifting*. *Adamant* is the ultimate in metallic hardness; it is impenetrable. Having reached the climax of her metal imagery, the poet achieves a rather remarkable transition to her concluding stanza. Still using the metal imagery, she brings in the word *thimble*. A thimble, though of metal, is associated with a particular type of *human* activity—an activity with which Emily Dickinson, most New England women of that time, and above all the dead woman, were familiar. The poet does not want to lose sight of the fact that this metallic thing "was" very recently a human being. Death affects only living things, and its relation to the living is what gives death significance. The *thimble* quite logically enables the poet to bring in the routine household work that the housewife will surely not neglect:

> Buzz the dull flies—on the chamber window—
> Brave—shines the sun through the freckled pane—
> Fearless—the cobweb swings from the ceiling—
> Indolent Housewife—in Daisies—lain!

The image of the buzzing fly is to appear again. She employs it here to indicate that one of the household chores is no longer performed. The fly can buzz with impunity, for there will be no one to swat him. The pane is freckled with dirt, and the cobweb dangles from the ceiling. Only a slovenly housewife would tolerate such things! Thus, with fine irony, Emily Dickinson makes her point. The woman is indeed lazy; she is an "Indolent Housewife" who has reached the height of inactivity: she is dead and buried.

Poems written before 1861 that fall into the third group, personifications of death, are not numerous.[8] They increase in later years, almost as if the longer she contemplated death the more intimate an acquaintance death became. There are, however, a few early poems in which she endowed death with human traits. Emily Dickinson's earliest known poem, dated March 4, 1850, was a valentine sent to Elbridge G. Bowdoin, a young man practicing law in her father's office. Apparently it was the custom to circulate ornate valentine verses among friends, and she did not intend her poem for anything more than lighthearted, good–humored verse. In this poem she chides Bowdoin for not having a sweetheart, saying that the earth was made for lovers, nothing was meant to remain single, and that even "death claims a living bride". Obviously she places this brief personification of death here as a mere passing remark, but it is interesting that it should appear in her earliest known poem.

A poem of about 1858, "I keep my pledge" (I, 46), little more than an exercise, personifies death by making it capable of calling or noticing. She wrote: "I was not called—/ Death did not notice me". Though she did not fully develop these early personifications, she was laying the groundwork for their effective use in her later poetry.

Another poetic "exercise" of about the same time, "If I should cease to bring a Rose" (I, 56), also personifies death. The poem itself is little more than a statement to the effect that if she ever ceases to honor friends and special occasions by gifts of roses "Twill be because *Death's* finger/ Claps my murmuring lip!" Thus Death is a person to the extent of having a finger. The fact that she underlined *Death's* indicates that she at least wanted its presence in the poem noted. In this poem she used one of her rhyme "echoes"—something that is not an exact, imperfect, suspended, or vowel rhyme, but still retains the barest hint of a rhyme. The words are *Commemorate–lip*, which have neither similar vowel sounds nor similar consonant sounds, but faintly echo each other by reason of the fact that both end in voiceless consonants. That this was intentional there can be little doubt, for she used this combination too often, and in places where one expects to find rhyme, for it to be accidental.

The most fully developed of her early personifications of death, one in which death takes on an actual personality, is "Dust is the only Secret" (I, 153), written about 1860. Emily Dickinson was so acutely conscious of death that she could sense its presence everywhere. As Richard Chase speculates, it had become a supreme cosmic force, an abstract power affecting all nature.[9] Obviously such an omnipotent and universal force would be worth understanding. It would be worth all of one's efforts to discover why such a force existed in the universe. The answers supplied by religion were unsatisfactory. Death as a "principle of nature" is an abstract concept, whereas Emily Dickinson's natural mode of thought was in terms of the concrete and specific—death as a *fact*. Her fondness for the concrete, her desire to discover the function of death personally, through her own existential experience, was at work here. If she could imagine death as a person, if she could picture it as something human, then perhaps she could come nearer to understanding its purpose. Personification of death was one of her ways of expressing the abstract in terms of the concrete.[10] This is the kind of "person" she found death to be:

> Dust is the only Secret—
> Death, the only One
> You cannot find out all about
> In his "native town."
>
> Nobody knew "his Father"—
> Never was a Boy—
> Had'nt any playmates,
> Or "Early history"—
>
> Industrious! Laconic!
> Punctual! Sedate!
> Bold as a Brigand!
> Stiller than a Fleet!
>
> Builds, like a Bird, too!
> Christ robs the Nest—
> Robin after Robin
> Smuggled to Rest!

She was investigating the *personality* of death. If she could locate *his* friends, question *his* fellow townsmen, or trace *his* history, perhaps she could understand *his* purpose in the world. But mystery still surrounds death, even though *he* is in personal garb. Information about *him* in his "native town" is scarce. *His* lineage is difficult to trace. *He* is a somewhat solitary character, preferring to remain rather aloof, finding "playmates" unnecessary. No one can remember *his* youth.

Although death's origins are obscure, certain of his personality traits are well known. In the third stanza, having found death's fellow villagers poorly informed, the poet has turned to a new source of information: her own personal observation. Death is industrious, a skillful and steady worker, not like the "indolent housewife" unable to perform her duties. Death, like Emily Dickinson herself, is anything but verbose. He is terse and to the point, too busy to waste words. He never misses an appointment. He is of a sober constitution, quiet and unruffled. Despite all these admirable qualities, however, there is something lawless in his nature; he is like a brigand or bandit, and moves with the swiftness and stillness of a fleet.

In the last stanza Emily Dickinson's religious background assumes a place. Death's "native town" knows little of him, whereas personal observation finds him with some desirable characteristics, but still a bandit. The investigation now reaches an impasse. Death is laconic and offers no hint of what happens to his hostages; the poet must fall back on religion for some answer, and it is the traditional one supplied by Christianity—death is not the end of life but the beginning, and "Christ robs the Nest" that death has built. Thus she closes the poem with a concrete image representing a religious concept.

Death as a person, of course, gave her no satisfactory

explanation of his existence, and she had momentary recourse to the Christian interpretation; yet she could not accept the religious orthodoxies of her day, and the Christian answer was for her a dubious one. Her personification of death was simply one of her ways of seeking to recognize it, to relieve her apprehensions about it, to familiarize herself with it, to understand it.

Examples of the fourth group of death poems, elegiac verse, are plentiful in the early years, and toward the end of her life she wrote almost nothing but elegies.[11] (*Elegy*, as used here, has nothing to do with any particular meter, but refers simply to those poems that offer a lament for, a tribute to, or in some way commemorate the dead.)

In many of Emily Dickinson's elegies one can identify the person for whom she intended the verse, but many more are so general that she appears to have written them for imaginary individuals. Though she sent a number of elegies as notes of sympathy to families who had suffered loss by death, her principal reason for writing was akin to that responsible for all of her death poetry: the need to understand death and to relieve doubts and insecurities associated with the phenomenon. The early elegies, like the early poems in the three previous groups, do not yet evidence much of that dramatic tension achieved in her later poetry. But these apprentice years were important—she was learning "Gem—Tactics—Practicing Sands".

"Morns like these—we parted" (I, 27), about 1858,

is an elegy addressed to an unidentified person, mentioned only in the poem as "she". It is a three–stanza poem, with exact rhyme throughout, in trochaic meter with the popular hymn book arrangement of alternately six and five syllables to the line. The poem, covering a single day, compares the process of dying to that of a bird learning to fly. In the morning the process begins, "Fluttering first—then firmer". This early elegy reflects Emily Dickinson's lifelong desire to hear some hint of immortality from the lips of the dying. But, the listener waits in vain:

> Never did she lisp it—
> It was not for me—
> She—was mute from transport—
> I—from agony—

This "transport" of the dying person, one infers, is caused by the knowledge that she will soon have an answer to the "riddle". As evening nears, the "bird" learns to fly; there is a rustling, "And this linnet flew!" Death is complete. Besides being a lament for the departed, this elegy also reveals Emily Dickinson's frustration over the silence of the dead. The poem itself is somewhat commonplace, and such a line as "To her fair repose" indicates the conventional nature of this early poem.

Another elegy of 1858, "Could live—*did* live" (I, 43), addressed to an unknown person, pays tribute to one who could die "With unpuzzled heart" because of a firm religious faith. Though Emily Dickinson could not personally accept orthodox religion, she never ridiculed an honest faith and had only high respect for firm religious convictions. In fact, one can detect a note of envy of those who were solidly convinced of immortality. The present poem carries such an implication. The person now dead could live and die, and "Could smile upon the whole/ Through faith in one he met not,/ To introduce his soul". He had never "met" Christ, but his faith enabled him to believe that through Christ he would be "introduced" into God's "elect".

"Taken from men—this morning" (I, 53), composed in 1858, another elegy to an unidentified person, includes three sets of images that Emily Dickinson was fond of applying to death. The first is battle imagery, used earlier to represent the struggling soul, the "Christian Soldier" fighting for Christ, and here also imbued with a religious connotation—albeit presented in a somewhat different manner. Here, the departed soul is "Met by the Gods with banners—/ Who marshalled her away—". *Banners* and *marshalled* convey the idea of a military force. Waving banners greet the accepted soul, and the Gods usher her on in triumph.

The concluding lines of the second stanza present the image of heaven as a house: "There must be guests in Eden—/ All the rooms are full". Very likely Emily Dickinson received this image from the Bible, perhaps from a line such as "In my Father's house are many mansions". It is also possible that her intense love for her own home gave rise to the feeling that heaven must be some kind of dwelling. Richard Chase, in fact, believes that "A house is one of our poet's favorite symbols of the mind".[12]

In the third stanza the "guests" have become "courtiers", and the "rooms" have become "kingdoms". Emily Dickinson frequently used some form of "royalty" image for the dead in heaven. It was her way of expressing the Puritan idea of reward "above" after a life of righteous lowliness and modesty on earth. In heaven, God's elect would indeed have the highest of all "rank". A later elegy to an "unknown", written about 1859, considers further the idea of honor and reward in heaven. Thus, in the poem beginning "Ambition cannot find him" (I, 68) the dead person is above and beyond ambition in the worldly sense, yet has achieved highest eminence in heaven: "Yesterday, undistinguished!/ Eminent Today".

In 1859 she composed a poem in memory of Charlotte Brontë. Since the latter had died in 1855, it is just possible that the poem was written on the fourth anniversary of her death. It is not an impressive poem, however, though the feeling is sincere, for Emily greatly admired Charlotte Brontë. The verse employs slightly irregular "common meter", and twice uses suspended rhyme. The first stanza gives an indication of the nature of the poem:

> All overgrown by cunning moss,
> All interspersed with weed,
> The little cage of "Currer Bell"
> In quiet "Haworth" laid.   (I, 148)

To represent the dead the poet again uses the image

of a bird, an image continued throughout the poem. "Currer Bell's" cage is discarded because "Currer Bell" has retired to "other latitudes" to escape the frost. But unlike the other migrating birds, she failed to return.

In April, 1860, Lavinia Norcross, the mother of Emily Dickinson's cousins Louise and Frances, died. Emily sent a poem to the cousins, obviously intending it to be nothing more than a note of sympathy, appropriate for their teenage ears. The girls doubtless appreciated the sentiments expressed, but an outsider would perhaps find them somewhat trite. Once more the poet compares the dead one to a bird, flown to another tree, but still able to look down with tenderness on her "sparrows". Here are the first four lines:

> Mama never forgets her birds,
> Though in another tree—
> She looks down just as often
> And just as tenderly   (I, 164)

For Emily Dickinson the years before 1861 were, in effect, years of apprenticeship, during which she was learning her "trade". Her technique, certainly, was not yet perfected, and most of the poems from this period are rather low–keyed productions as compared to those which follow. There is, however, an occasional glimmer of the lightning thrusts to come. The potentials are there, ideas are opening and expanding, and even her technique shows signs of the impulse to experimentation. The next period, 1861 to 1865, marks the summit of her achievement.

V

Emily Dickinson's
Most Creative Period, 1861-1865

❖

THE YEARS OF EMILY DICKINSON'S GREAT-
est productivity coincided with the carnage of the Civil
War. Considering the intensity of her interest in death
even in peace time, it can be safely assumed that the
war heightened her awareness of death still further, and
that this heightened awareness was largely responsible
for increased literary activities. During just one of the
war years, 1862, she produced the sizable total of 366
poems.[1] However, these years were important for much
more than mere quantity of production. Her creative
skill also reached its height during this period. The
poems of Civil War years fall naturally into the four
categories listed in the preceding chapter, beginning
with poems about death and immortality.

Emily Dickinson's continuing Puritan anxiety about
the possibility of not being included among the "elect",

and her consequent preoccupation with the theme of death, are both apparent in the poem beginning "You're right—'the way is narrow' " (I, 234), written in about 1861. The first stanza is unusual in that each of the four lines contains a quotation from the Bible:

> You're right—"the way *is* narrow"—
> And "difficult the Gate"—
> And "few there be"—Correct again—
> That "enter in—thereat"—

The words in quotation marks are slightly inaccurate citations from Matthew 7:13-14, but the meaning is essentially the same: that the way to Christ is a straight and narrow road, and few reach the goal. In the second stanza the poet drops the biblical language and substitutes words usually associated with commerce or finance:

> '*Tis* Costly—So are *purples*!
> 'Tis just the price of *Breath*—
> With but the "Discount" of the *Grave*—
> Termed by the *Brokers*—"*Death*"!

The sudden juxtaposition of language from the Bible with language used in commercial enterprise is highly effective and especially so considering the fact that the commodities involved are things ordinarily considered to be literally beyond price—breath and life. What does one receive for such a price?

> And after *that*—there's Heaven—
> The *Good* Man's—"*Dividend*"—

> And *Bad* Men—"go to Jail"—
> I guess—

Still using words associated with monetary transactions, she finds "Heaven" to be a "Dividend" for the "Good Man". The "Bad Man" is locked up. The Puritan notion of heaven as a reward for the deserving is expressed in terms of business enterprise.

Another poem of 1861, "Why—do they shut Me out of Heaven?" (I, 248), deserves mention as an illustration of the anxiety caused by her belief that she had been denied membership in the "elect":

> Why—do they shut Me out of Heaven?
> Did I sing—too loud?
> But—I can say a little "Minor"
> Timid as a Bird!

This stanza reveals her ability to embody thought in image. The Transcendental "bird", because she sings too loudly, cannot gain entrance to the Puritan heaven. For Puritans, humility, lowliness, and a sense of man's dependence were (and are) incompatible with spontaneity and the self–sufficiency of the private man. The poet's image reflects the tension generated by these poles.

One of the most overtly religious poems ever written by Emily Dickinson is "Tie the Strings to my Life, My Lord" (I, 279), dating from about 1861. In it she openly announces that she is seeking a religious life and renouncing her former ways. The Puritan preoccupation with religion again mirrors its effect on the poet. Unable to accept orthodox methods, she sought a personal relationship with God, seeking acceptance through private channels. In this particular poem she uses the image of a coach-and-horses to indicate the departure of the "poetic I" from the life she used to live. She recognizes that her choice is not easy, and she requests: "Put me in on the firmest side—/ So I shall never fall". The meter is a combination of trochaic and dactylic feet. Emily Dickinson uses exact rhyme, vowel rhyme in *go–do*, and suspended rhyme in *fall–hill*. Her experimentation expands.

Because Emily Dickinson was not a consistent or systematic thinker, many of her expressed attitudes probably reflected no more than her mood at the time of writing. For her, the world was not a well–ordered place, and she could find no doctrine or philosophy that would satisfactorily explain the fact of death. Having found that "wholes are not below", the best she could do was to hope that in some hypothetical life after death the pieces of the puzzle would fall into place. She did recognize evil in the world, and its principal form was death. Her feeling that she was constantly "molested" by death and immortality caused her to give way to resignation and even despair, on occasion, as it did when she wrote the following poem, in or about 1862:

> I reason, Earth is short—
> And Anguish—absolute—
> And many hurt,
> But, what of that?

> I reason, we could die—
> The best Vitality
> Cannot excel Decay,
> But, what of that?
>
> I reason, that in Heaven—
> Somehow, it will be even—
> Some new Equation, given—
> But, what of that?   (I, 301)

It is a poem of despair, the despair making a logical progression from one state of being to another, each represented by one of the three stanzas. Here is that passionate engagement in "extreme situations" so characteristic of the existentialist. When anguish becomes absolute in this life, what of it? Anguish will leave when death comes, for decay will conquer both anguish and vitality. And what of death? Some adjustment will be made in heaven and things will be put in balance. But after this third stage, is there another place to go? The despondency becomes complete, as the poet questions whether even heaven can adjust evil.

The repetition used in this poem is an unusual device for Emily Dickinson. The first two words of the first lines in each stanza are identical, and the question, "But, what of that?" ends each stanza. Her own sense of despair quite likely dictated this repetition, the dirge-like monotony of the repeated words serving to reinforce her sense of hopelessness and futility.

Continuing inability honestly to feel "converted" led her to seek some hint of immortality from observation of the dead. Thus, in 1862 we find her writing:

> It is dead—Find it—
> Out of sound—Out of sight—
> "Happy"? Which is wiser—
> You, or the wind?
> "Conscious"? Wont you ask that—
> Of the low Ground?
>
> "Homesick"? Many met it—
> Even through them—This
> Cannot testify—
> Themself—as dumb—   (I, 417)

Once again she uses the pronoun *it* to convey the neuter
quality of the dead. Yet, if the dead person's soul is
immortal, surely some semblance of human qualities
must remain. But how can one locate something "Out
of sound—Out of sight"? Are the dead happy? The wind
knows as much about it as we. Immortality must include consciousness, yet the dead show no more awareness than the ground. The grave refuses to reply. But
there are those who have met "it". They should be
able to testify. Unfortunately, they are also dead and,
of course, are mute. The effort is again frustration. She
proved nothing and found no answer, and yet, through
her poetry, Emily Dickinson was testing her ideas on
death. Her method was not to state profound truths in
verse but to test certain thoughts verbally under the
pressure of the connotations of the words in the poem.

Emily Dickinson's attitude toward death did indeed
influence her poetic style. Her basic attitude may be de-

scribed as one of fear, uncertainty, doubt, and apprehension. How did this attitude affect her poetry? In the first place, her constant awareness of death lends an atmosphere of tragedy to her serious poetry. The recognition of death as an evil in the world provides the sense of conflict necessary to tragedy. Death, the cat, plays with man, the mouse. Since the duration of life is uncertain, man must live his life in a hurry, as if to outrun death. Her poetry reflected this feeling of haste and urgency. She wished to express what she had to say in the shortest way possible. Impatient with punctuation, she resorted to the dash—and used even this inconsistently, sometimes to cut a phrase in two, at other times in place of a comma, or a period, or question mark.

Emily Dickinson did not pretend to understand the complexities and contradictions present in the world because of death. And yet they remained a source of constant and worrisome concern. Her poems are attempts to express the complexities and contradictions through words. Hence, in the context of a poem, one word modifies and qualifies another. Certain words clash, and at times the like unites with the unlike. With little or no thought of "proving" anything, she was letting clusters of words, and the connotations resulting from one word playing against another, reflect the intricacies and paradoxes of the universe. In a sense, the *words* themselves are the spontaneous and active agents in her poetic universe.

To illustrate: Puritanism led her to believe that man was in a precarious position, but Transcendentalism

claimed that man had unlimited capacities. What, indeed, she might ask, was man's true relation to deity?
In a poem from 1863 we see how she let a particular arrangement of words consider the problem:

> It's easy to invent a Life—
> God does it—every Day—
> Creation—but the Gambol
> Of His Authority—   (II, 724)

The poet starts from observation: birth and death seem
to follow no recognizable pattern; God snuffs out life as
quickly and as often as He creates it. The process must
be *easy*, and something that is easy gives rise to the notion of a frolic or a *gambol*. Is she then somewhat shock-
ingly associating a stern Puritan God with a frolic? This
implication, brought about by the pressure of one word
on another, is unmistakable. The second stanza reads:

> It's easy to efface it—
> The thrifty Deity
> Could scarce afford Eternity
> To Spontaneity—

The fact that God so often snuffs out life gives rise to
the notion that He must be *thrifty*—thrifty, that is, of
eternity. God is omnipotent, but the Transcendental
man, too, has a will and may feel called upon to protest
God's choices:

> The Perished Patterns murmur—
> But His Perturbless Plan
> Proceed—inserting Here—a Sun—
> There—leaving out a Man—

The protest is a mere murmur, of course, and has little or no effect. In the first stanza the poet found the God of her observation to be a rather frisky God, perhaps acting out of whim. But Puritan tradition affirmed that God, being a purposeful being, *must* have a "Plan". It is "Perturbless" because the murmur of the "Perished Patterns" is not heard. Once again the poet relies on observation to discover God's plan, a plan which, ironically, is no plan at all. To insert here a sun and there leave out a man is whimsy. Religion, philosophy, reason, observation, all at last prove inadequate in discovering essence. Her stance is existential.

In the last stanza there is an example of deliberate omission of an auxiliary verb. In "His Perturbless Plan Proceed", what appears to be a lack of agreement between subject and verb is actually not. If one imagines *does* before *Proceed,* the difficulty vanishes. Omitting such verbs was a habit with Emily Dickinson.

Puritanism taught her that this world was a mere phase, a test for the coming life eternal, and that one did not really begin to "live" until after death—one, that is, who was fortunate enough to be among God's "elect". She tests this idea in a four–line poem written in about 1864:

> A Death blow is a Life blow to Some
> Who till they died, did not alive become—
> Who had they lived, had died but when
> They died, Vitality begun.   (II, 816)

The idea is examined in terms of paradox. Common sense conceives of life and death as mutually exclusive

states. The assertion that "A Death blow is a Life blow"
is apparently contrary to usual opinion. Not only does
death give life, but life would have given death. The
resolution of the paradox lies in the qualifying word
some. Interpreted in the light of her religious background, the *some* would be those received by God after
death, who had they lived would have fallen out of
God's grace.

Emily Dickinson looked upon death as the most crucial experience in life, as the focal point of all of the
incongruities of the universe, as the center from which
radiated all the contradictions and intricate complica-
tions of existence. If one could but observe from that
center, he could look in all directions. This idea is
tested in a poem written about 1864, "The Admirations—and Contempts—of time" (II, 906). The idea of
time she associated with evil. Time was important because death was here. Eternity and immortality, she was
taught, are the goals of every Christian life; since they
exclude time, it must be something undesirable. But
the nearest she could come, in this world, to a place
where time did not matter was at the grave. To the one
buried, of course, time was over; to the observer, it
seemed insignificant for the moment. She found that
"The Admirations—and Contempts—of time—/ Show
justest—through an Open Tomb—/ The Dying—as it
were a Hight [*sic*]/ Reorganizes Estimate". This height,
which is out of time, affords a new perspective. One
sees things that he did not see before—the radii are more
distinct viewed from the center:

'Tis Compound Vision—
Light—enabling Light—
The Finite—furnished
With the Infinite—
Convex—and Concave Witness—
Back toward Time—
And forward—
Toward the God of Him—

Again joining terms that are usually considered mutually exclusive, *finite–infinite, convex–concave, back–forward*, the poet finds a vision *compounded* of these unlike elements, granted only at this particular spot of death because time has been stopped. The poem achieves a sense of unity through references to time in the opening line and at the end. For a brief moment she stood in the center, between past and future, looking back at time and forward toward God. Here was the mystical experience granted to the "persona" of the poems that had been denied to Emily Dickinson of Amherst through orthodox religious channels.

Illustrations from the second group, comprised of poems dealing primarily with the physical aspects of death, are plentiful in these years, and include some of her best executed poems. In 1861 she composed the following two–stanza poem:

I like a look of Agony,
Because I know it's true—
Men do not sham Convulsion,
Nor Simulate, a Throe—

The Eyes glaze once—and that is Death—
Impossible to feign
The Beads upon the Forehead
By homely Anguish strung.   (I, 241)

Since she could not, by observation, test the truth of
Transcendental doctrine, Puritan creed, or the sermons
which she heard in church, Emily Dickinson did not
find many certainties in life. But her observations of
people in the process of dying did furnish her with one
virtual certainty—that actual physical pain and the
point beyond pain, death, were not likely to be feigned.
This direct, raw experience was unmistakably "authen-
tic". There was no need to rely on any assumption or
preconceived notion about truth. The intensity of concrete experience needed no abstract philosophy to give
it life. Highly sensitive to sensations of all sorts, she was
especially impressed by intense ones connected with
acute pain shortly before death.[2] Thus *agony, convulsion, throe,* and *anguish,* while not things to be desired,
are at least unmistakably what they are. Typical of her
paradoxical findings is that the two things impossible to
feign are, in a sense, at opposite extremes. Man is perhaps never so aware that he is a living, physical organism as when he is suffering intense physical pain, intense and unpleasant stimulation of the senses. From
one viewpoint, then, this condition is the apex of life.
The other condition impossible to sham is death—apparently a complete absence of sensation. Emily Dickinson was never sure of the purpose of death, but she
could always be positive of its presence.

Another poem of 1861, "A clock stopped" (I, 287), translates the cessation of life into the image of a clock that has stopped:

> A Clock stopped—
> Not the Mantel's—
> Geneva's farthest skill
> Cant put the puppet bowing—
> That just now dangled still—

The image is quite appropriate for her, since she felt so strongly the tie between time and mortality. When death comes, time departs. Furthermore, she invariably associated motion with life, stillness or pause with death. When the puppet was *bowing*, it had motion and was alive. Now that it can no longer move, now that it is *still*, it is dead.

In the second stanza, reference is made to the clock as a "Trinket", and it is now little or nothing more than that, since it can no longer run. The only indication that the clock is capable of feeling, like a human being, is that just before it stopped, "The Figures hunched, with pain". One final convulsion, then it "quivered out" of life "Into Degreeless Noon". The hands of the clock are together at noon; there are no degrees between the hands on the circle. Not only time has stopped, but all measurement has stopped, and the pause and stillness are complete.

Neither the "Shopman" nor the "Doctor" can *stir* "This Pendulum of snow" back to life. Snow and frost she often used as symbols for death. A dying body loses its warmth, becomes cold, and loses color, taking on two of the attributes of snow. "Pendulum of snow" again shows the poet's fondness for joining disparate objects, and for a purpose. One associates *Pendulum* with motion (for Emily Dickinson a symbol of life), and yet the poem is a description of death. *Snow* she associated with death; therefore, to signify that the pendulum was motionless, she wrote "Pendulum of snow".

The concluding stanza conveys the sense of frustration over the silence of the dead. The shopman importunes in vain; only a "cool–concernless No" stares out at him from the dial, "Decades of Arrogance between/ The Dial life—/ And Him". The dead's refusal to respond is akin to arrogance.

Thus Emily Dickinson metaphorically describes the death of a person. She does not use metaphor in "There's been a Death, in the Opposite House" (I, 389), written about 1862, and gives a realistic account of certain evidence of the aftermath of death. The viewpoint is that of one who is observing the activities in a nearby house soon after someone has died there. The fact that the observer is not actually a member of the household lends a certain impersonality and objectiveness to the observation. The source here is surely from personal experience, from her witnessing the effects of death as felt by neighbors in Amherst.[3] The house itself gives off the atmosphere of death, and the observer knows someone has died "by the numb look/ Such Houses have—always". There is increased activity, as if the survivors wish to compensate for the complete stillness of the dead one. The verbs *rustle, drives, opens, flings*, and *hurry* carry this sense of motion. There is an unusual effect in this poem that deserves comment: in spite of all this activity, with which it is usual to associate sounds of some kind, the whole poem conveys an impression of silence, as if the figures were participating in a dumb show. Yet nowhere is it stated that the actors are silent, or that there is no sound. Evidently the observer is at some distance from the house, too far to hear the sounds; and since the reader knows nothing except what he is told by the observer, he too is unable to "hear" sounds that would accompany the activities described. Here is a striking example of how Emily Dickinson not only let words in the poem qualify one another but let the entire context of the poem exert an influence on particulars. The poem is, indeed, a triumph in restricted point of view.

In the third stanza the evidence of recent death is rather grim:

> Somebody flings a Mattrass [*sic*] out—
> The Children hurry by—
> They wonder if it died—on that—
> I used to—when a Boy—

Flings is appropriate, carrying the impression that something extremely unpleasant is discarded with haste. Again, the poet uses the pronoun *it* to convey the neuter quality of the dead.

Other figures follow the neighbors in the silent procession: the minister—acting as if the house were his, the milliner, and the "Man of the Appalling Trade".

One knows from this evidence that the funeral, the
"Dark Parade", will soon follow, and that the panto-
mime will end.

About 1862 she composed "I heard a Fly buzz—when
I died" (I, 465). The impressions made upon Emily
Dickinson in the presence of the dying had been intense, and in this poem the fictive "I" speaks in anticipated retrospect of her own sensations during death:

> I heard a Fly buzz—when I died—
> The Stillness in the Room
> Was like the Stillness in the Air—
> Between the Heaves of Storm—

Again the poet presents the ever persistent idea of *stillness* associated with death, emphasizing the stillness by
contrasting it with noise. One would be highly conscious of stillness between claps of thunder. "Stillness
in the Air" further connotes the sense of a stifling atmosphere and, in the context of the poem, suggests the
difficulty the dying one has with breathing. "Heaves of
Storm", besides being appropriate for its contrast, further carries the idea of dying throes in the word *heaves*.

The second stanza focuses attention on those present
in the room of the dying person:

> The Eyes around—had wrung them dry—
> And Breaths were gathering firm
> For that last Onset—when the King
> Be witnessed—in the Room—

Unquestionably, Emily Dickinson had been exposed to

copious tears shed by mourners in the presence of the dying. In this poem the point is reached where the flood has been "wrung" dry. The moment of death is nearing, and once again the poet uses battle imagery, carried by the word *onset*. Death is personified as a *King*, an example of the images of royalty that she often used in connection with death and immortality.

The third stanza returns to the dying person, who wills her keepsakes, "and then it was/ There interposed a Fly". The final stanza pursues the course of the fly, taking up where the first stanza began, lending unity to the poem:

> With Blue—uncertain stumbling Buzz—
> Between the light—and me—
> And then the Windows failed—and then
> I could not see to see—

The conventional view would assume that the "uncertainty" and the "failure" lay, not with the buzz of the fly and with the window, but with the dying person, gradually losing consciousness. From the viewpoint of the one dying, however, the objects of his vision—the fly and the window—are fading, not he.

"Blue buzz", an example of synesthesia, is appropriate and logical within the context of the poem, since a dying person would be quite likely to experience a confusion of senses. Also, of course, the color blue suggests the color of the fly—the central image in the poem. In an earlier poem the fly that "buzzed with impunity" represented household duties that the "indolent housewife" would now shirk. This connotation is still present here. Furthermore, the "buzzing" of the fly, emphasizing the stillness of death, also represents the confusion and inefficiency of the weakening senses of the dying. One further suggestion, not pleasant to consider, but almost unavoidable, is the association of flies with carrion. The inescapable fact is that the dying one will soon be a corpse.

Emily Dickinson often approached death from the viewpoint of a tough–minded observer. She made a determined effort to avoid emotion or sentimentality, to view the dying as if witnessing a process about which she had no preconceived notions. Such an approach is exemplified in another poem, from about 1862:

> 'Twas warm—at first—like Us—
> Until there crept upon
> A Chill—like frost upon a Glass—
> Till all the scene—be gone.   (II, 519)

One of the most persistent impressions from her observation of the dying was that the dead were *cold*. In fact, the first three stanzas of this poem liken the process of dying to the process of freezing. Again using the pronoun *it* in reference to the dying person, she indicates how the course of dying is gradual, like that of freezing. At first warm, the dying one then felt a *chill*, a chill which crept. Incidentally, here is an example of one of Emily Dickinson's omissions. She leaves out the pronoun *it* that would ordinarily follow *upon*.

In the closing line of the first stanza, there is a curious switch of points of view from that of the observer to that of the dying. The chill is like frost on window glass which obscures the scene, obscures the scene not for the observer but for the dying. Death approaching is the chill that gradually weakens the vision of the dying person whose view is becoming more obscured by "frost" forming on the "windows" of his eyes. The last two lines thus become meaningful.

The process of freezing advances in the second stanza: "The fingers grew too cold/ To ache". Numbness replaces pain, as in the case of one freezing to death.

The freezing is complete in the third stanza: "It crowded Cold to Cold". Emily Dickinson, once again finding the silence of the dead exasperating, allows this physical coldness to turn into pride. Acutely sensitive to connotations, she associates cold with pride, shifting from a purely physical sensation to a quality of personality: "It crowded Cold to Cold—/ It multiplied indifference—/ As Pride were all it could".

This silence, this refusal to communicate, the dead one maintains to the very end. "It" has congealed, it is heavy like ice, and its stubborn pride persists. The body is lowered into the grave, and "It made no Signal, nor demurred,/ But dropped like Adamant". The "frozen" body is as hard as adamant, in appearance at least, and the pride is as impenetrable.

In a poem from 1862, written in "short meter", Emily Dickinson focuses attention on one of the organs of sensation, the eye, in the moment of death:

> I've seen a Dying Eye
> Run round and round a Room—
> In search of Something—as it seemed—
> Then Cloudier become—
> And then—obscure with Fog—
> And then—be soldered down
> Without disclosing what it be
> 'Twere blessed to have seen—   (II, 547)

Here is close observation—the eye rapidly shifting, then gradually filming over, then the final shutting of the lid. There is the implication that the eye, like Emily Dickinson, was searching for some sign or some presence which would indicate that this was not the end. The word "blessed" carries a religious overtone, suggesting that the dying eye was searching for some sign of "grace".

The cemetery adjacent to the Dickinson orchard gave Emily ample opportunity to study a final resting place of the dead. "Who occupies this House" (II, 892), from 1864, metaphorically describes the cemetery as a town. Though the words *cemetery* and *grave* do not appear in the eight-stanza poem, there is no mistaking the subject. The poet reasons that the occupant of the "house" must not be well known, since he finds it necessary to write his name and age upon the "door". There is skillful use of paradox in the poem. One usually associates a town with activity, but of course in this "town" stillness predominates. It was this very quality of stillness that attracted the first settler: "A Pioneer, as/ Settlers often do/ Liking the quiet of the Place/ Attracted more unto". Emily Dickinson characterizes the citizens with black humor: the town is "Distinguished for the gravity/ Of every Citizen". She appropriately concludes the poem with a reference to the "stranger" whose "house" first attracted her notice.

In about 1864 she composed a poem about the moment between life and death, the moment when life hangs in the balance—the very second when the scales will be tipped one way or the other. " 'Twas Crisis—All the length had passed—/ That dull—benumbing time/ There is in Fever or Event" (II, 948) describes that long period of waiting for a crisis in terms of space and time. The poet uses the word *length* in an unusual fashion. *Length* is not often thought of as something that *passes*. Yet, as she uses the word here, it is something that *passed* in time. There is also the connotation here of the *length* of life—a length of thread on a spool is unwound, a weak place is reached, and the moment will decide whether the thread will snap or continue to unwind without a break. Will Clotho continue to spin her thread, or will Atropos use her "abhorred shears"? *Length* also carries the connotation of boredom or tedium, which is exactly what she wishes to convey and does so overtly in the "benumbing time" of waiting for the crisis. Here she uses the device of slightly dislocating the word from its dictionary meaning to fit the context of her poem, a device with which she achieves some of her best results. She saw complexities and contradictions in the world, emphasized by her religious doubts and her anxiety over death. She also saw words leading in many directions, with a complex of meanings. Perhaps if she could give these words full play, letting them exert pressures and qualifications upon each other, if she could make apparent incongruities work toward a finer texture of meaning, then perhaps she could accept the incongruities present in the universe as only apparent ones, capable of being reconciled.

In the final three stanzas of the poem, the elements in the drama become animate. The "instant" actually becomes a living thing, "holding in it's claw/ The privilege to live/ Or warrant to report the Soul/ The other side the Grave". The term *warrant* suggests the influence of the legal terms that she had probably heard her father use.

The muscles grapple with the approaching heaviness descending on the body, and again Emily Dickinson makes use of her favorite words "Adamant" and "lead" to indicate the weight of death and also the condition of the person who is becoming as unfeeling as adamant. The fight is still on, however, and "The Spirit shook the Adamant/ But could not make it feel". The "Second" has become alive in the final stanza; the drama is brought to a close:

> The Second poised—debated—shot—
> Another had begun—
> And simultaneously, A Soul
> Escaped the House unseen—

To the end of her life, Emily Dickinson sought for some evidence of the "spirit" in the "body". But just as this "soul escaped the House unseen", the evidence was always to escape her.

Poems in the third group, personifications of death, reach full development during these years. The inevitability of death is the theme of a poem written about 1862:

> It's coming—the postponeless Creature—
> It gains the Block—and now—it gains the Door—
> Chooses it's latch, from all the other fastenings—
> Enters—with a "You know Me—Sir"?
>
> Simple Salute—and Certain Recognition—
> Bold— were it Enemy—Brief—were it friend—
> Dresses each House in Crape, and Icicle—
> And Carries one—out of it—to God—   (I, 390)

One of the poet's methods of gaining some insight into the nature of death was to endow it with certain qualities of human beings. In the present poem, although she allows death to speak, she preserves the mystery surrounding death by withholding from it a fully human personality. Death is still a "Creature", and the pronoun *it* indicates the separation between death and the world of living men and women. Because death is laconic, one has difficulty determining whether it is a friend or an enemy. This uncertainty expresses precisely Emily Dickinson's own feelings toward death. Not being certain of its purpose, not being certain of immortality, she could never be certain of death's intentions. Death stays only long enough to decorate the house with his favorite colors, black and white, then leaves with one of the occupants. The fact that death will carry one to God still does not stamp him as a friend. The final judgment is yet to come, and the soul presented to God may be denied membership in the "elect".

The meter of this poem varies greatly from the strict regularity of the hymn book. The lines contain mixed feet of iambic, trochaic, and dactylic. The rhyme is suspended: *Door–Sir, friend–God.*

Frost is a recurrent symbol for death in Emily Dickinson's poetry. In a poem of 1862 this element in nature, this impersonal force present in the universe takes on life. Frost, or death, becomes:

> A Visitor in Marl—
> Who influences Flowers—
> Till they are orderly as Busts—
> And Elegant—as Glass—   (I, 391)

Frost is a "Visitor" on earth; he is not a member of the human race, and the implication is that he should not be here. He is an evil force, and if things were what they ought to be, this force would not be present. His influence is particularly insidious, because the surface appearance presents a fine show—"elegant" and "orderly".

Death further ingratiates himself with those he interviews by pretending to be a lover. His romantic nature prefers the night, "and just before the Sun—/ Concludes his glistening interview—/ Caresses—and is gone". The final stanza indicates the result of the "interview":

> But whom his fingers touched—
> And where his feet have run—
> And whatsoever Mouth he kissed—
> Is as it had not been—

The surface appearance of his influence—elegant, glistening, orderly—conflicts with the reality, which is total destruction. In an effort to understand death as an abstract force in the universe, Emily Dickinson chose to present death in concrete images, in this case as an insidious visitor.

Two poems written in 1862 deserve brief mention as reflections of the religious aspect of her interest in death. Both poems contain personifications of death, but they are incidental and not fully developed. In "I read my sentence—steadily" (I, 412), the "persona" is preparing her soul for the worst possible sentence it could receive—which by implication would be exclusion from heaven. If this is to be her sentence, then she wants to become as familiar as possible with death. To think of death as a friend is difficult, but to do so might relieve the shock of actual meeting. Then perhaps the agony of the soul would not be novel:

> But she, and Death, acquainted—
> Meet tranquilly, as friends—
> Salute, and pass, without a Hint—
> And there, the Matter ends—

The second poem, "Triumph—may be of several

kinds" (I, 455), personifies death as an "Old Imperator" who at times is overcome by faith. Emily Dickinson's inability to experience conversion left her aware of the insecurity of her faith, and the possibility that God would not accept her increased her anxiety over death. The closing lines of this poem suggest that her preoccupation with death was partly caused by a fear of rejection by God. The greatest triumph comes to those "who pass/ Acquitted—from that Naked Bar—/ Jehovah's Countenance".

In "Because I could not stop for Death" (II, 712), written about 1863, the "persona" has become familiar enough with death to imagine him as a friend, a friend indeed because he conducts her to eternity. While Emily Dickinson was never fully convinced of immortality, neither was she completely despairing of its possibility. Her feelings would waver from belief to doubt to denial. At times she could think in this manner: if death turned out to be a coachman for eternity, what would he be like? She tests the idea in the poem:

> Because I could not stop for Death—
> He kindly stopped for me—
> The Carriage held but just Ourselves—
> And Immortality.

Busy with her household chores, the speaker, the "I" of the poem, has no time for death, but he is so considerate and polite that he "kindly" stops for her. (There is no irony intended here: if death were conducting her toward eternity, she would indeed consider him kindly.)

Because such things as *haste, labor,* and even *leisure* all involve time, she puts away these for death. As they drive out of the world of time, she observes the scenery:

> We passed the School, where Children strove
> At Recess—in the Ring—
> We passed the Fields of Gazing Grain—
> We passed the Setting Sun—

The strenuous activity of the children, by contrast, heightens the fact that the observer is dead, or at least passing out of life. And it is the grain that is gazing, not the dead or dying rider in the carriage! The sense of sight she will bequeath to the grain.

In spite of the fact that they are headed for eternity, death still seems cold. Emily Dickinson could rarely allow an opportunity to pass without emphasizing the chill of death. Death, although "kindly", had not warned his passenger of the dampness, and she came dressed in a "Gossamer Gown" and a shawl of thin tulle.

She observes a final scene in their journey—the grave: "We paused before a House that seemed / A Swelling of the Ground". It is significant that they only *paused.* The implication is that the grave was not their final destination. That it was not is made clear in the final stanza. Here the poet writes that it was centuries ago "I first surmised the Horses Heads / Were toward Eternity". And so the trip ends.

A poem written about 1863, "Bereaved of all, I went abroad" (II, 784), is unusual in that it personifies the grave itself. No poem expresses more clearly how thoughts of death constantly pursued Emily Dickinson. Persistently molested by the grave, the "persona" travels to a "New Peninsula", only to find that the grave had already arrived, had in fact

> Obtained my Lodgings, ere myself—
> And when I sought my Bed—
> The Grave it was reposed upon
> The Pillow for my Head—

The grave is sharing her room and even her bed—a most unwelcome intimacy. This strange bedfellow is awake before her in the morning; she tries to lose it in the crowd or the sea and finally she does manage to lose the grave itself, "but the Spade/ Remained in Memory". The implication is that by great effort she has momentarily managed to dislodge the image from her mind; but the spade, the instrument of the grave, is still there, ready at any time to dig another grave, to present her with another roommate.

In "Color—Caste—Denomination" (II, 970), written about 1864, the poet once again contrasts time and death. Time is an aristocrat who concerns himself with color, caste, and denomination. Death is a democrat, whose "large—Democratic fingers/ Rub away the Brand". Death may "put away/ Chrysalis of Blonde— or Umber", but they will emerge as "Equal Butterfly". This poem shows her reaction from the Puritan notion of the "elect". The Puritan concept of heaven is not a democratic one, as far as admission is concerned. Once the soul gets through the gates, then perhaps there is equality, but the gates themselves are not open to all. The poem reflects an influence of Transcendentalism. If all men are potentially divine, if all have a spark of divinity within them, then all are capable of emerging into the "butterfly" state. This frequent preoccupation with time, one is tempted to add, also suggests her kinship with modern existentialist thought.

Two poems in this third group are interesting because of their form, that of the dialogue. In about 1864, following in the tradition of the debate, though presumably not actually indebted to that popular medieval literary type, she wrote "Death is a Dialogue between/ The Spirit and the Dust" (II, 976). The image is somewhat confused here since in the poem the figure of death is not actually the dialogue but a participant in it. The final two lines of the first stanza read: " 'Dissolve' says Death—The Spirit 'Sir/ I have another Trust' ". Death really takes the role of the "Dust" in the dialogue. The discourse becomes indirect in the second and concluding stanza:

> Death doubts it—Argues from the Ground—
> The Spirit turns away
> Just laying off for evidence
> An Overcoat of Clay.

This argument reveals Emily Dickinson's own tension created over the conflict that she saw between observed fact and certain abstract beliefs not capable of being tested by observation. Her direct observation of death pointed toward the dismal but apparently unavoidable conclusion that death was final. Her personal desire, of course, was for evidence of some afterlife in which she would be included. Death argues from the *ground*—from matter, from observed fact, from the viewpoint of a scientist. The "Spirit" refuses to accept this evidence as conclusive, claiming a life beyond matter, and to prove his point sloughs off the coat of clay. The "Spirit" in the dialogue represents Emily Dickinson's desire to believe in eternity, the "Dust" represents the observed facts. This clash was to continue throughout her life.

About 1865 she again personified death as a participant in a dialogue:

> Said Death to Passion
> "Give of thine an Acre unto me."
> Said Passion, through contracting Breaths
> "A Thousand Times Thee Nay."
>
> Bore Death from Passion
> All His East
> He—sovreign as the Sun
> Resituated in the West
> And the Debate was done.   (II, 1033)

The fact that Emily Dickinson was acutely conscious of the presence of death in the world did not make her any the less conscious of life. If anything, her awareness of death made her more anxious to live the kind of life she selected. Her seclusion, her concentration on the small area of life in her immediate environment, was a conscious choice on her part. This deliberate choice, this "negative capability", reflects her modern existentialist thought. She did not spend her time mourning over the presence of death, but rather in trying to understand it. Her concern over death was not morbid; she was not "half in love with easeful death" or with the grave and, in fact, had a great zest for life. The traditional Romantic "death-wish" was not involved. T. W. Higginson, in his meeting with her in 1870, reported her as having said, "I find ecstasy in living; the mere sense of living is joy enough".[4] The poem above reflects this passion—this desire for the sense of life. And "Passion" will not weaken itself merely because death requests it to do so.

Several connotations of the word *Passion* increase the subtle force of this poem. On one level the poet no doubt intended the word to convey nothing more than the "ecstasy" found in "the mere sense of living". Death cannot daunt this intense feeling of being alive. The word also conveys the idea of love, in the sense of affection for one of the opposite sex. Many of her love poems imagine the lovers being reunited in heaven, actually consummating in heaven the love that had been unfulfilled on earth. The concluding stanza of the present poem suggests this image. Death takes from Passion "All his East", the word *East* implying morning or youth. Undaunted, true passion "resituates" itself "in the West", the *West* implying old age, or actual death, if one accepts her idea of the lovers meeting in heaven.

A further possible connotation of the word *Passion* is its religious meaning—Christ's suffering on the cross. Emily Dickinson's religious background makes this con-

notation a likely one. Christ's suffering and physical
death on the cross, the poem suggests, did not destroy
His eternal life; death did not actually conquer. Dickinson implies that it was Christ's character as a person,
not the fact that He was the son of God, which allowed
Him to rise from the dead. She was to write later,
" 'Twas Christ's own personal Expanse/ That bore him
from the Tomb" (III, 1543). In this religious sense,
Passion conquered death.

The fourth group of poems from this period, the elegies, include tributes to both identified and unidentified people, and perhaps even imaginary ones. In 1862
she wrote three poems in memory of Elizabeth Barrett
Browning, who had died June 30, 1861. Emily admired
Mrs. Browning, perhaps as much for the drama of her
life, and the mere fact that she was a woman, as for her
poetry. But her tributes to Mrs. Browning are not
among Emily Dickinson's better poems; they are too
effusive and lacking in the emotional restraint characteristic of her most successful work. In the first, "Her—
'last Poems'—/ Poets—ended" (I, 312), she writes in an
almost too persistent and regular trochaic meter. Her
adulation is unrestrained:

> Silver—perished—with her Tongue—
> Not on Record—bubbled other,
> Flute—or Woman—
> So divine—

The poem continues with its praise, remarking that any

tribute conferred will be dull "On the Head too High
to Crown". Dickinson closes the poem with a reference
to Robert Browning, reminding herself that her own
sorrow must be nothing compared to that of the husband: "What, and if, Ourself a Bridegroom—/ Put Her
down—in Italy?"

The second tribute, "I went to thank Her—/ But
She Slept" (I, 363), has more simplicity and restraint,
and conveys a sincere sense of personal loss, a deep regret that it is too late for Elizabeth Barrett Browning
to hear her "thanks". The speaker in the poem imagines
visiting the tomb, "a funneled Stone". If she could have
made the trip when the "Anglo-Florentine" was alive,
the voyage would have been short; finding her dead,
the "turning back—'twas slow". The word *slow* seems
well–chosen to express her poignant regret that she
cannot now thank Mrs. Browning for her poetry. Re-
luctancy to accept her death, lack of vitality caused by
the sense of loss, an actual physical reaction in the slow-
ing down of motion—which for Emily Dickinson would
be the ultimate in sincerity of grief, being "impossible
to feign"—all these are conveyed in the word *slow*.

The third poem that she wrote as a tribute to Elizabeth Barrett Browning, the one beginning "I think I
was enchanted" (II, 593), is primarily an account of
how Mrs. Browning's poetry affected Emily Dickinson.
The poem does not refer to Mrs. Browning by name,
but only as "that Foreign lady". The effect is described in terms of a religious, mystical experience.
The speaker "read that Foreign Lady":

> And whether it was noon at night—
> Or only Heaven—at Noon—
> For very Lunacy of Light
> I had not power to tell—

The phrase "Lunacy of Light" clearly indicates a sudden, mystical experience. The "persona" was indeed enchanted: bees became butterflies, butterflies became swans, and nature's "meanest tunes" became operas. The terms become increasingly religious; she finds the days adorned "As if unto a Jubilee/ 'Twere suddenly confirmed". The word *confirmed* clearly has religious connotations, and Emily Dickinson wrote in the word *Sacrament* as a suggested change for *Jubilee*. The next stanza continues the use of religious words:

> I could not have defined the change—
> Conversion of the Mind
> Like Sanctifying in the Soul—
> Is witnessed—not explained—

Conversion, sanctifying, soul, witnessed all carry religious overtones. The fact that Emily Dickinson was never able to experience a religious conversion makes this language especially interesting. Poetry filled the gap left by her inability to "experience" religion through the orthodox channels of her day. Her remarks to T. W. Higginson concerning the nature of poetry are germane here:

> If I read a book [and] it makes my whole body so cold no fire ever can warm me I know *that* is poetry. If I feel physically as if the top of my head were taken

off, I know *that* is poetry. These are the only ways I
know it. Is there any other way.   (II, 473–74)

This is the language of religious experience. There is
little question that poetry, for her, served as a "substitute" for religion and that a religious fervor motivated
her own writing.

The poem to Mrs. Browning concludes by referring
to the experience as a "Divine Insanity", and suggests
what cure to use if the "persona" is ever in danger of
losing her "insanity". The antidote is to turn

> To Tomes of solid Witchcraft—
> Magicians be asleep—
> But Magic—hath an Element
> Like Deity—to keep—

The "Tomes of solid Witchcraft" are the writings of
Mrs. Browning, and she is the magician who is now
asleep. The magic, her poetry, will keep, even though
she is "asleep".

We have seen that the carnage of the Civil War led
Emily Dickinson to intensify her effort to understand
death, to consider and reconsider her ideas in the increased poetic output of these years. Indirectly the war
influenced all the poetry from this period, but at least
four of her poems, all composed in about 1862, were
directly inspired by it.

"They dropped like Flakes" (I, 409) compares the
mass loss of life on the battlefield to the falling snow-
flakes, stars, or petals blown from a rose by a strong June
wind. Carrying out the analogy to its logical conclusion,

one might infer that those killed in action would also vanish as quickly as melting snow, falling stars, or rose-petals lost in the grass. This idea is, in fact, conveyed by the first two lines of the second and final stanza: "They perished in the Seamless Grass—/ No eye could find the place". The final two lines, however, revert to the tra-ditional Christian conclusion: "But God can summon every fact/ On his Repealless—List". Once again ob-served fact and religious faith clash, and though siding with religion in this instance, she cannot wholly deny her sense of the horrible finality of death. The phrase "Repealless List" carries this idea. The list is final, un-alterable, irrevocable.

The poem beginning "It dont sound so terrible—quite—as it did" (I, 426) she very likely wrote upon learning of the death of Frazer Stearns, son of the pres-ident of Amherst College and a close friend of the Dick-insons.[5] The poem represents an attempt to accept the loss and to adjust the grief caused by the shock of his death. It is in a very loose, irregular meter, one that perhaps reflects the poet's own bewilderment at the time. It does employ rhyme—exact, suspended, and identical rhyme. The first stanza shows how the impres-sion registered in her mind: "I run it over—'Dead,' Brain, 'Dead.'/ Put it in Latin—left of my school—/ Seems it dont shriek so—under rule". In order to break the repetition of the words in her brain, she tries to dis-lodge them by shifting them to another language. The unruly emotion she tries to subdue by subjecting it to "rule", to the order of language.

She imagines her grief as a physical object, as something having weight and size:

> Turn it, a little—full in the face
> A Trouble looks bitterest—
> Shift it—just—
> Say "When Tomorrow comes this way—
> I shall have waded down one Day".

Characteristically, she treats something immaterial, in this case grief, as though it were matter. She will *turn* her trouble, she will *shift* it. Viewed from another angle, the object will look smaller. She tries to console herself with the knowledge that time will dim the grief. But she also knows that time will "take its time" doing so, slowly. The struggle even to move at all through the days she conveys by the verb *waded*. This unexpected use of the word enhances its effectiveness. A verb usually associated with a specific type of physical motion—movement through water—she uses to convey the slowness and difficulty of passing through time. Wading can be a slow, tedious, tiring process, and she knows that "wading" through a single day will be just this difficult.

She is aware that time will accustom her to what is now new, and she reasons that

> It's shrewder then
> Put the Thought in advance—a Year—
> How like "a fit"—then—
> Murder—wear!

In this stanza are two examples of the poet's habit of

condensing her verse through omissions. She omits *to*
between *then* and *Put*, and omits the auxiliary *will* before *wear*. This peculiar habit contributes to the sense
of urgency in her poetry, as if in her eagerness to make a
point she has skipped certain words along the way. An
element of rather grim irony is present in this stanza,
as she realizes that time will eventually lessen her grief,
while also realizing that time will never, no matter how
slowly, restore the young man's life. *Should* one adjust
to death in war? Is it *proper* to make a nice "fit" out of
something that is actually a form of murder? In the
word *murder* she bitterly sums up her attitude toward
war.

The poem beginning "It feels a shame to be Alive"
(I, 444) does not commemorate any one person but
rather honors all who have died in the war. A sincere
tribute to those who have put away their lives "In Pawn
for Liberty", it questions whether those at home are
worthy of such a sacrifice, whether the price is not too
great:

> The price is great—Sublimely paid—
> Do we deserve—a Thing—
> That lives—like Dollars—must be piled
> Before we may obtain?

The "Thing" is liberty, but the poet feels shame in
being alive, doubting as she does that "we that wait"
are worth the destruction of the "Enormous Pearl"—
life—which is "dissolved" in "Battle's—horrid Bowl".
She pays a final tribute by seeing something godlike in

the sacrifice. The men who die "Present Divinity". It is appropriate and in good taste that she chose to write this "hymn" in praise of the dead in a strictly regular hymn book "common meter".

The fourth poem directly inspired by the Civil War is in memory of a particular person, probably a Francis H. Dickinson of Belchertown, who was killed in 1861 at the battle of Ball's Bluff, on the Maryland border.[6] The first stanza reads:

> When I was small, a Woman died—
> Today—her Only Boy
> Went up from the Potomac—
> His face all Victory   (II, 596)

The boy and his mother are reunited in heaven. The poet does not know "If pride shall be in Paradise", but in her own mind the mother and son proudly "Pass back and forth". *If* heaven is heaven, *if* there is any justice, she is sure that "Bravoes—/ Perpetual break abroad/ For Braveries, remote as this/ In yonder Maryland".

These poems directly inspired by the war, though perhaps not Emily Dickinson's greatest, do show that she was not a recluse who took no interest in the national calamity. Her world was small, to be sure, but she was by no means insensible to the tragedy of war and the sufferings of others.

An elegy to an unidentified person, beginning "We Cover Thee—Sweet Face" (I, 482), was composed in 1862. It is written in "short meter", and the frequent use of the pronouns *thou* and *thee*—they appear seven times in this twelve–line poem—shows the influence of the language of the Bible and the hymn books. The poet wishes to assure the dead person that the living cover her face not because they tire of it, "But that Thyself fatigue of Us". No doubt Emily Dickinson had observed the custom of covering the face of the dead, and had questioned its purpose. Of one thing she was sure: it was not because the living did not wish to view the face until the last possible moment. The entire tribute revolves around her desire to assure the dead one that it is with the utmost reluctance that they turn away:

> We follow Thee until
> Thou notice Us—no more—
> And then—reluctant—turn away
> To Con Thee oer and oer—

An unconventional tribute, it is an improvement over many of her somewhat trite earlier ones.

The poem "If anybody's friend be dead" (II, 509) is addressed not to those who are dead but to those who have lost a friend. Certain details associated with the dead friend bring the sharpest anguish in remembering —how he walked, his dress, a prank, a smile, a chat. Once again the blame for breaking the lines of communication is placed on the dead rather than the living, who can still remember when they "chatted close with this Grand Thing/ That dont remember you". The dead forget, not the living. In her eagerness to receive one sign from the dead, one hint to relieve her own anxiety concerning death and immortality, she reproaches the dead for their refusal to communicate. Though the simple things remembered about the dead friend are painful to recall, the source of greatest anguish is reserved for the climax in the last stanza. The dead friend is beyond invitations, interviews, and vows. He is past these things, but he is also "Past what Ourself can estimate—/ That—makes the Quick of Wo!" It is this mystery, this doubt of what happens after death that is the real woe.

In a rather grim poem from 1862, "Her Sweet turn to leave the Homestead" (II, 649), the poet metaphorically describes the death of a young girl in terms of a wedding. This poem derives in part from Emily Dickinson's observations of the various trappings and activities associated with deaths and funerals which, in many ways, are like those of weddings. Thus:

> Her Sweet turn to leave the Homestead
> Came the Darker Way—
> Carriages—Be sure—and Guests—True—

It was an extravagant affair, and "Never Bride had such Assembling". Kinsmen and guests were gathered there in honor of the "bride". The poem returns from this flight of fancy, however, to the grim reality that the girl is, after all, dead. Anyone who asks for her hand in marriage "shall seek as high/ As the Palm—that serve the Desert—/ To obtain the Sky". The insistent observation that the dead are still and motionless appears in the line, "Distance—be Her only Motion". Emily

Dickinson's continuing sense of frustration in having received no communication from the dead, she now transfers to the suitor who, if he wishes to receive a "Nay—or Yes" from the young girl, "must have achieved in person/ Equal Paradise". It is difficult not to see Emily Dickinson as the young girl in the poem. None of Edward Dickinson's children actually left "the Homestead". Emily was now thirty-two and certainly aware that "Her Sweet turn to leave the Homestead" would come "the Darker Way".

Though "Her final Summer was it" (II, 795) is ostensibly written to some unidentified person, the reader feels, again, that Emily Dickinson is picturing herself. Continually aware of death's nearness, she lived in haste and wrote with urgency. As she told T. W. Higginson, "Shortness to live has made me bold" (II, 480). During the "final summer" of the poem, the "girl's" friends could see a certain "industriousness" in her, thinking only that somehow "A further force of life/ Developed from within". However, "When Death lit all the shortness up/ It made the hurry plain". She "hurried" because of "shortness to live". When there is nothing left of the girl but the marble tomb, "Her Carrara Guide post", the friends then realize the cause for her haste:

> When duller than our dullness
> The Busy Darling lay—
> So busy was she—finishing—
> So leisurely—were We—

These poems of Emily Dickinson's middle period, from 1861 to 1865, reveal the poet at the height of her creative powers. The Civil War, Wadsworth's departure to California, her own recognition of the flux and relativity of the human lot, her taut suspension between Puritanism and Transcendentalism, her full commitment to the study of death—all contributed to the flowering of her mature art during this period.

A poem written about 1864, memorializing the death of an aunt, Mrs. Joel W. Norcross, deserves mention as an expression of Emily Dickinson's despair at the prospect of never learning, on earth, the ultimate fate of those who die. The poem begins "From Us She wandered now a Year" (II, 890) and concludes that those on earth must remain ignorant of "that Etherial [*sic*] Zone/ No Eye hath seen and lived". The only definite and conclusive statement that one can make is "We only know what time of Year/ We took the Mystery". To the very end, death was to remain a mystery. There is a note of despair here, almost a kind of grim resignation, and for this reason the poem will serve as a good transition to those of 1866 and after, in which she dwelt increasingly on the apparent hopelessness of ever solving the "riddle" in this life.

Poems of Her Later Years

❖

DURING THE LAST TWENTY YEARS OF HER life, Emily Dickinson wrote fewer poems than she had during her five most productive years. Whereas in 1862 she composed 366 poems, the most she was ever to write in a single year after 1865 was fifty, in 1873. She wrote some excellent poetry during her late period, but much of it lacks the intensity of the poems from 1861–1865. The decline in productivity did not result from any lessening of her anxiety over death; the later poems indicate that it was still very much with her. But in her most highly productive years, 1861–1865, she seems to have seriously depleted her reserves of strength and energy.

A further reason for lessened output was a purely practical one. Her mother became paralyzed in June, 1875, and from that time until her death in November, 1882, remained an invalid.[1] Most of the responsibility of caring for the mother fell upon Emily, who naturally had less time to devote to her poetry. In 1884 Emily herself became a semi–invalid and was able to write only at infrequent intervals.[2] During the last two years of her life she composed but twelve poems.

Her deep interest in death and immortality did not abate, and a substantial number of her post–1865 poems on death fall into this grouping.

In considering immortality, Emily Dickinson could at times wonder whether such a condition would actually be desirable. Immortality implied eternity, and eternity she associated with infinity. At the same time, religion told her that the life to come far surpassed any life here on earth. She tests this idea in a poem of 1870, beginning "The Life we have is very great" (II, 1162). This life is great, but "The Life that we shall see/ Surpasses it, we know, because/ It is Infinity". Infinity is without limits of any kind, immeasurable and boundless. In such a condition one could behold "all Space", and see "all Dominion". But is this kind of existence desirable? The poem concludes: "The smallest Human Heart's extent/ Reduces it to none". The implication is that boundless, immense, immeasurable immortality might be frightening and overwhelming. It also might not be human enough. The "Human Heart's extent" reduces infinity to nothing. If death destroys the "human heart", if heaven has no "humanity", then perhaps immortality is not desirable.

A penciled draft written about 1872 is interesting in that it contains lines borrowed from another poet—a rarity in her work. The poem also expresses her great desire to believe in some kind of immortality. It is a four–line stanza:

> If my Bark sink
> 'Tis to another sea—
> Mortality's Ground Floor
> Is Immortality—   (III, 1234)

Mable Loomis Todd and Millicent Todd Bingham point out that "If my bark sinks, 'tis to another sea" is a line from "A Poet's Hope" by William Ellery Channing.[3] The poem reflects Emily Dickinson's interest in Transcendentalism as a counterbalance to Puritanism. If all men had a spark of the divine, then the doctrine of the "elect" would be invalid. The final two lines are rather unusual in that they picture immortality, ordinarily associated with "height", as a "Ground Floor". The explanation is that probably she wished to be consistent with the image of the *sinking* vessel, which was *lowered* into immortality. Also, of course, if the poet looked upon the ground floor as the foundation, then one could suppose that she was picturing immortality as the basis for life, in the Puritan sense that to achieve life eternal is man's *only* reason for being on earth.

Emily Dickinson's feelings of religious insecurity intensified as she grew older. In a poem of 1873, "Who were 'the Father and the Son'" (III, 1258), she is almost bitter in reproaching God for not having made His nature clear when she was a child. As the years pass, she becomes increasingly more resentful of the ever–present anxiety of religious uncertainty, expressing this resentment in her poetry. The "persona", in this poem assuming the role of first person plural, recalls an early desire to "know God":

> Who were "the Father and the Son"
> We pondered when a child,
> And what had they to do with us
> And when portentous told
>
> With inference appalling
> By Childhood fortified
> We thought, at least they are no worse
> Than they have been described.

The "inference appalling" can only mean that the child listened to sermons on the sternness of the Puritan God, who saves a select few and allows others to perish. A child's mind would magnify the grimness.

The third stanza implies that "the Father and the Son" might themselves answer, if today the "child" repeated the question—but the child, now grown, has no more heart left for it: "had they the felicity/ When we desired to know,/ We better Friends had been, perhaps,/ Than time ensue to be".

The next stanza clearly expresses the distress Emily Dickinson suffered from the instability of her religious faith. One believes "entirely" only once, and from that time "Belief, it does not fit so well/ When altered frequently". This line, especially, reveals the nature of her own feeling. Her great desire to be "saved" was at odds with her inability to accept conversion; the Puritan insistence on man's dependency conflicted with the Transcendental concept of his self–sufficiency. Her feelings on immortality ranged from acceptance, to doubt, to denial. Her belief was, indeed, "altered frequently".

The poem ends in despair. Even "if we achieve" heaven, the fact that we have "shunned" it so often will make us almost "ashamed/ To own the Miracle".

Emily Dickinson released the resentment built up against her religious background in an eight–line poem written in 1873, "Is Heaven a Physician?" (III, 1270). It is unusual in its bitterness, for it was not often that she expressed her sense of injury so openly:

> Is Heaven a Physician?
> They say that He can heal—
> But Medicine Posthumous
> Is unavailable—
> Is Heaven an Exchequer?
> They speak of what we owe—
> But that negotiation
> I'm not a Party to—

After one is dead, what good is medicine? Why could not God use His healing powers here on earth as well as in heaven? The speaker would have welcomed a little balm to apply in this world, particularly when she attributed the source of the trouble directly to the "physician" himself.

Once again the poet applies a term associated with finance to heaven. The metaphor is the height of incongruity—comparing the ultimate goal of the spirit, heaven, to a treasury. But the comparison is effective because of its shock. Puritan religion told her that she owed to herself and to God: humility, renunciation of worldly gains, a persistent seeking after "grace". Not only should she owe herself to God, but she should dedicate her entire life to Him. The insistence on what one *owed* sounded very much like a business arrangement. Very well, she would use commercial terms in voicing her resentment. She would have no objection to paying an honest debt, incurred by her voluntary action in entering into a business partnership. But not having been consulted in this arrangement, she would be no *party* to "that negotiation". Heaven had not asked for her signature; consequently, she should be under no obligation. An open protest against God's refusal to reveal His purpose openly, the poem is at the same time a reaction against her Puritan background.

At times, Emily Dickinson could feel that death was "all". Her personal observations of the dying had failed to support belief in any form of existence after death. This sense of the finality of death she expressed in "Lain in Nature—so suffice us" (III, 1288), written about 1873. The poem is an interesting example of how she could employ the special terminology of an activity with which she was familiar—in this case, gardening—to express her thoughts on death.

> Lain in Nature—so suffice us
> The enchantless Pod
> When we advertise existence
> For the missing Seed—

Maddest Heart that God created
Cannot move a sod
Pasted by the simple summer
On the Longed for Dead—

(Incidentally, the usage of her day justifies what appears
to be an error in her use of *lain*. As Whicher has pointed
out, Webster's *American Dictionary* [1847], which is
the one she used, gave as one of the meanings for *lie* "to
be reposited in the grave",[4] the sense in which she is
using the word in this poem.)

Terms associated with gardening are *Pod, Seed,* and
sod. If one supplies the auxiliary *must* before *suffice,*
the meaning then becomes "the empty pod must suffice us when the seed is missing". If the seed is missing
and irrecoverable, the pod is all that is left. Yet this is
small satisfaction, for the pod is not capable of being
enchanted into life.

By implication, the "Longed for Dead" are like the
pod without its seeds, that is, a dry vessel that had for-
merly held life. Once more, Emily Dickinson gave vent
to her sense of frustration over the isolation of the dead,
their complete insulation from human contact, a bare
layer of earth as effective a barrier as a mountain of steel.
She suggested *soldered* as a change for *Longed for,*
strengthening the interpretation that the poem expresses her bafflement and anger over the silence of the
dead.

There is an implicit dualism running through Emily
Dickinson's poetry, often beneath the surface, but at
times rising into view. Unlike Emerson, she placed no

credence in any "bridge" between "reality and the soul". And, unlike Whitman, she asserted no belief in any mystical "merging" of the body and spirit, subject and object, man and nature. She never strained after that monistic identity between man and the external world. Her outlook remained that of a modern existentialist. Always there remained that structural gap between thought and existence. She was conscious of two worlds, the world of mind and the world of matter, the world of "ideas" and the world of "facts".[5] By observation and experience one may test certain "facts" about man's existence, but neither observation nor experience is of value in testing the validity of certain religious aspirations, hopes, or fears. These two areas of life very often come into conflict, and much of her anxiety arises from the clash. Perhaps something in human nature seems, at times, to demand unity, and to be basically opposed to any form of dualism. On occasion Emily Dickinson would attempt artistically to resolve this dualism by expressing ideas or the ideal in terms of sensations. Such attempts, of course, did not remove the apparent "fact" of dualism in the real world, and thus did not effectively resolve the conflict in her own mind.

One possible "solution" is frankly to accept the dualism, and in a poem dating from about 1874 she adopts this course, by giving recognition to the two separate spheres of matter and mind:

> Two Lengths has every Day—
> It's absolute extent
> And Area superior
> By Hope or Horror lent—   (III, 1295)

There is the actual physical length of the day, the world
"outside", apparently made up of matter, known by a
"subject" through the organs of sense. The "Area su-
perior/ By Hope or Horror lent" is the world of the
mind, the world of the "subject" itself, conscious of but
somehow distinct from the world "out there".

Significantly, in the final two stanzas she considers
eternity and death, showing the close relationship, in
her life, between the philosophical problem of dualism
and problems arising from her contemplation of death
and immortality. The second stanza reads:

> Eternity will be
> Velocity or Pause
> At Fundamental Signals
> From Fundamental Laws.

Before discussing this stanza, we should notice a variant
reading for the final two lines: "Precisely as the Candi-
date/ Preliminary was".

Here, again, is an odd blending of Puritanism and
Transcendentalism. Emily Dickinson persistently associated lack of motion, stillness, or *Pause* with death.
Conversely, motion, movement, or *velocity* meant life.
She says that eternity will be one of the two, velocity or
pause, life or death. From the Puritan standpoint, eternity will be "life" or "death" according to whether or
not one has been "saved". The word *Candidate* in the
variant reading has religious overtones implying *candidate* for membership in God's "elect". And yet in the
last stanza—

> To die is not to go—
> On Doom's consummate Chart
> No Territory new is staked—
> Remain thou as thou art

there are Transcendental overtones. Man himself will determine whether or not he will have "velocity" or "pause". There is no "new Territory", no sudden reception of the "elect" arbitrarily selected by God, into a new territory of bliss. Man's "own personal expanse" will determine whether he will continue to "move" after death or whether he will "stop". The stanza also implies that the problem of dualism will be "solved" in "eternity".

An extant worksheet draft, written in pencil by Emily Dickinson about 1877, is an open admission of her absorbing interest in the question of immortality. Religious insecurity originally motivated her to consider death and immortality as a major theme in her poetry. As time passed and as her poetic "investigations" multiplied, as she continued to test her ideas in poetry and to relieve certain tensions by so doing, she discovered that she had developed an interest not confined to religion. The very fact that she never became fully certain of the existence or of the nature of a life after death served to hold her attention. If she had ever pieced together the puzzle, if she had solved the "riddle", its fascination would have been lost. Without ever losing her religious motivation, she had added a further dimension to her interest, one consisting of a rather impersonal in-

tellectual curiosity. Furthermore, she was able to separate the one from the other. The first stanza of the
worksheet draft illustrates how she kept her curiosity
alive:

> How Human Nature dotes
> On what it cant detect.
> The moment that a Plot is plumbed
> It's meaning is extinct—   (III, 1417)

Though she employs the phrase "Human Nature", she
is obviously speaking of her own personal experience.
She approached her study of death and immortality
with unrelenting fervor; yet she was never able to "detect" conclusive answers to her questions. What was
the purpose of death in the world? Was death final or
was it the beginning? Were only a chosen few "saved",
or were all "saved"? The "Plot" was never "plumbed".

In the last stanza the poet makes explicitly clear
which unfinished "Plot" she feels to be most worthy of
respect:

> Of subjects that resist
> Redoubtablest is this
> Where go we—
> Go we anywhere
> Creation after this?

Emily Dickinson did not want to be skeptical of immortality.[6] She desperately desired to believe that there
was something after death. This desire is evident in a
poem from about 1882, "Of Death I try to think like
this" (III, 1558). The word *try* in the opening line indi-

cates the effort the speaker is making to convince herself that death is not the end. Being lowered into the ground is like being lowered into a well, and "The Well in which they lay us/ Is but the Likeness of the Brook/ That menaced not to slay us,/ But to invite by that Dismay". Death is present to make heaven seem that much better; it is not here merely to "slay us". The "brook" of death guards the desired "Purple Flower" on the other side. Though the brook may frighten a child by its "roaring", the bold will leap across and clutch the flower. She *tried* to think of death as a flower on "the other side" that would be worth the leap.

Emily Dickinson could not sustain this mood for long, however, and in an eight-line poem written in 1884 we find her questioning the worth of the "flower":

> The going from a world we know
>   To one a wonder still
> Is like the child's adversity
>   Whose vista is a hill,
> Behind the hill is sorcery
>   And everything unknown,
> But will the secret compensate
>   For climbing it alone?   (III, 1603)

Resentment is unmistakable. Before, she expressed interest and even fascination in the unfinished "plot". Now she questions whether unraveling it could ever be worth the loneliness and struggle of the reading. Her observation of the silence and isolation of the dead could not fail to impress her with the loneliness of death. Everyone dies alone. Will the sorcery "behind the hill" be worth the lonely, difficult climb? As Emily Dickinson approached the end of her life, the burden of being "molested" by the question of immortality became heavier.

After 1865 there is a decided decline in the number of poems that fall into the second category (poems treating the physical aspects of death). Perhaps this type of poem, requiring close observation of the dying, the dead, and the aftermath of death, took too much of her energy. Thomas H. Johnson has aptly termed her view "clinical" and "medical".[7] In her almost clinical approach to the study of death in many poems, she examined, with microscopic intensity, the details of dying, and quite probably this super–realism became somewhat too grim to dwell on as she herself grew older. Furthermore, her primary motive in observing the dying and the dead had been the hope of receiving some hint of what happened after death. Having always met with silence, she may possibly have come to realize the futility of death watches. Yet Emily Dickinson by no means abandoned the physical aspect of her subject, for she continued to write of it as late as 1884. Though fewer in number, her later poems on the physical appearance of death are among the best poems written in these years.

"The Bustle in a House" (II, 1078), written in about 1866, is yet another consideration of the effects of death on routine household activities. The poem derives considerable force by its use of sudden and unexpected juxtapositions. *Death, love,* and *eternity* are united with the homely activities of *sweeping* and *putting away*. Not given to philosophic abstractions, the poet hoped for some understanding of death by considering this force in the concrete, existential terms that she did understand.

> The Bustle in a House
> The Morning after Death
> Is solemnest of industries
> Enacted upon Earth—
>
> The Sweeping up the Heart
> And putting Love away
> We shall not want to use again
> Until Eternity.

One does not ordinarily consider the bustle of household activities to be the "solemnest of industries/ Enacted upon Earth", but in the context of the poem the metaphor is meaningful. The qualification that the activity takes place "The Morning after Death" is, of course, what makes it "solemnest of industries", and the bustle is indeed an *industry*, requiring the utmost efforts of those left behind. Though few feel like tending to the mundane chores of the daily routine, the tending must go on.

The impact of the death on those in the house is highlighted by such homely activity. The bustle, activity, and industry of the living make the absence, silence, and stillness of the dead that much more noticeable. Further, such routine activity as "sweeping" and "putting things away", carried on day after day, becomes almost automatic, requiring little actual thought. What began as conscious effort and industry has now become automatic routine, etherizing the sense of loss, the shock of death giving way to the numbness of mechanical motion.

Paradoxically, though the activity is routine, it is not routine. The living are well aware that this day is not just another day, though they are trying to go through the motions as if it were. This awareness is made obvious by the last stanza. Along with dust, they are "Sweeping up the heart". In "putting away" the household items in their proper places, they are also "putting Love away". Like storing winter clothes for which they will have no use until cold weather, the family puts away love that "they shall not want to use again/ Until Eternity".

This uniting of the like with the unlike, the joining of the "thimble" with "eternity", the habit of letting words and phrases qualify, reinforce, or contradict one another is typically Dickinsonian.

"The last Night that She lived" (II, 1100), also composed in 1866 or so, was almost certainly based on first-hand observation. Thomas H. Johnson points out that in May, 1886, Laura Dickey, daughter of Mr. and Mrs. L. M. Hills, died at her parents' home, situated next to the Dickinsons' on the east.[8] Emily was probably there. Instead of describing the effects of death on the living the morning after death, as did "The Bustle in the House", this poem considers the effects immediately before, during, and shortly after death. Once more, the presence of death makes an ordinary situation seem extraordinary:

> The last Night that She lived
> It was a Common Night
> Except the Dying—this to Us
> Made Nature different
>
> We noticed smallest things—
> Things overlooked before
> By this great light upon our Minds
> Italicized—as 'twere.

As the poet had written earlier, "Death reorganizes estimate". Under the powerful floodlight of death, one sees things unseen before, and also from a different perspective.

Passing in and out of the sickroom, the observer begins to feel "a Blame/ That Others could exist/ While She must finish quite/ A Jealousy for Her arose". Judging from similar situations as depicted in other poems, one infers that the "Blame" is directed more toward God than toward the living—blame for not allowing them full knowledge of His plan. The observer is "jealous" of the one about to die, for shortly she will "walk within the riddle". The moment of death is approaching, and those present in the house "waited while She passed—/ It was a narrow time—/ Too jostled were Our Souls to speak". The poem reverses the usual roles of the dying and the living. The living are still; it is they who *waited*. The dying girl has motion; she *passed* and, in passing, *jostled* the souls of the living because of the *narrow* time. *Souls* and *time*, abstractions both, the poet knocks down to size, places them into another frame of reference, the world of sensation, where they become concrete objects that can be *jostled*, that can be described as *narrow*; concepts thus become physical objects in her poetry, objects that can be turned, handled, examined from all sides. Once the girl is actually dead, however, the living resume their active roles, and the dead one is now motionless and passive:

> And We—We placed the Hair—
> And drew the Head erect—
> And then an awful leisure was
> Belief to regulate—

Immediately after death, after friends have positioned and adjusted the body, "an awful leisure" replaces the tension and strain of waiting for death. One imagines, however, that the "Bustle in the House" will soon replace the "awful leisure".

Emily Dickinson's insistent observation that the dead are cold and immobile appears once again in "Too cold is this/ To warm with Sun" (II, 1135), written about 1868. The impersonality of the dead is again indicated by means of the pronoun *this*. The dead person is not only too cold ever to be warmed, but

> Too stiff to bended be,
> To joint this Agate were a work—
> Outstaring Masonry—

The lifeless body is as cold, as hard, as inflexible, and as silent as agate. The poet conveys the complete finality of death by emphasizing its complete lack of motion and the impossibility of any future resumption of motion. "To joint" the agate would bring back motion— life— but where is the mason who can work this miracle?

The final four lines switch from the image of an agate to the image of a husk, emptied of its kernel:

> How went the Agile Kernel out
> Contusion of the Husk
> Nor Rip, nor wrinkle indicate
> But just an Asterisk.

Once again the poet's fondness for flowers and plants influences her selection of images. The puzzle of death, the eternal mystery surrounding it she conveys by the disappearance of the kernel. The kernel of a nut leaves some trace or mark of its exit, but not the life escaping from the body. The only sign is the asterisk—the mark by names in a list to indicate the decease of the person so designated. This is the only "contusion".

Not until about 1881 could Emily Dickinson again bring herself to write a poem concerned primarily with the physical demise of the body, and on this occasion it was to emphasize the vast distance that separates the dead from the living:

> Oh give it Motion—deck it sweet
> With Artery and Vein—

Upon it's fastened Lips lay words—
Affiance it again
To that Pink Stranger we call Dust—
Acquainted more with that
Than with this horizontal one
That will not lift it's Hat—   (III, 1527)

Again she uses the neuter pronoun *it* to indicate the dead person's complete removal from the world of *he's* and *she's*. The corpse, once a living, moving organism, is now neither fish nor fowl. There is irony in the use of the imperative: "Give it motion—deck it sweet". The directive has more of the nature of entreaty than of command, and of course the poet is aware that her plea cannot be fulfilled, but again she points to three attributes of the dead that have persistently impressed her— their lack of motion, their coldness, and their silence: the qualities that distinguish the dead from the living. If the body could regain *motion, warmth* through artery and vein, and the power of *speech*—then it would no longer be dead.

The lifeless body will shortly mingle with the dust and, in its intimacy, will in a sense be betrothed to dust, or death. The poem closes with yet another expression of resentment against the dead. They have remained eternally obstinate in their refusal to communicate. The dead *could* make some sign if they but would, but apparently they would rather not. Thus, the poet does not say that the horizontal one *cannot* lift its hat, but that it *will not*.

Emily Dickinson never stopped hoping to receive

some hint from the dying as to the nature of death. As
late as 1884, two years before her death, she was still
seeking an answer from the dying in "Still own thee—
still thou art/ What surgeons call alive" (III, 1633). At
the very moment when life is leaving the body, "slipping—slipping I perceive/ To thy reportless Grave",
the speaker strives to receive some sign which would
clarify the grave:

> Which question shall I clutch—
> What answer wrest from thee
> Before thou dost exude away
> In the recalless sea?

The words *clutch* and *wrest* indicate the desperation of
her desire. Once in the grave, the dead can issue no report; once in the sea of death, the dead can receive no
summons to return. Emily Dickinson's Puritan background, her religious trouble at Mount Holyoke, and
the overwhelming presence of her father all emphasized
her "unregenerate" state. Yet, she might have reasoned,
if observation did nothing to support accepted religious
beliefs, then perhaps the orthodox religion of her day
was wrong. If, through personal observation of the dying, she could find evidence refuting traditional beliefs,
then her own fears, doubts, and concern might vanish;
and so to the end she continued her close, analytical observations of the dying.

Late examples falling into the third category, personifications of death, are not so plentiful as those in the
category to follow—the elegies. Furthermore, one finds

fewer fully developed personifications than in the earlier works. Still, the device of giving death human characteristics continued to be one of the important methods of the poet in her unrelenting quest for knowledge
of death.

A poem from 1869, "The Frost of Death was on the
Pane" (II, 1136), considers the possibility of fighting
death, of hunting him, and of tracking him to his den.
Again using the image of frost for death, Dickinson
gives him the human quality of speech. Death declares
his intentions and announces, "Secure your Flower".
The friends of the intended victim try to prevent the
advance of death, placing themselves in between her
and death, "Yet easy as the narrow Snake/ He forked
his way along/ Till all her helpless beauty bent".

Emily Dickinson sometimes felt helpless when con-
fronting the inscrutability of death, but this helpless-
ness gave way to anger: "And then our wrath begun/
we hunted him to his Ravine/ We chased him to his
Den". The attempt, of course, was futile. To do battle
with this powerful, unknown force seemed unfair; and
her sense of being trapped in a bewildering universe
she expresses in the concluding stanza:

> We hated Death and hated Life
> And nowhere was to go—
> Than Sea and continent there is
> A larger—it is Woe

In terms of this poem, death is an evil force in the
world, something to be tracked down and killed like a
wild beast. The battle is unequal, however, and this in-

equality and injustice is the root of her sense of cosmic "Woe". Indirectly, the poet is again blaming God for not giving knowledge of His "plan" and, in particular, knowledge of the purpose of death and what lies beyond.

An eight-line poem beginning "Not any higher stands the Grave" (III, 1256), composed in about 1873, again personifies death as a "Democrat". To observe that death takes all, king as well as peasant, is neither new nor startling, and the idea would be likely to occur naturally to almost anyone observing the qualities of death. But the poem contains more than this platitude. The first stanza notes that the grave accepts equally heroes and plain men, youth and age. The verb that she uses to close the poem deserves some special comment. The final three lines read:

> The Beggar and his Queen
> Propitiate this Democrat
> A summer's Afternoon—

The verb *propitiate* reflects Emily Dickinson's own mixed feelings about death. She may have observed that death is a "Democrat", but she also has observed that he is a *demanding* one. Not only does he *accept* all equally, but he *demands* all. He is something that requires *propitiation* and appeasement; man must cater to his tastes. In this light he turns out to be not a "Democrat", but a tyrant and an autocrat. The poet has subtly altered meanings by allowing one word to shift the meaning of another within the context of her poem.

A poem written in about 1875, "How soft this Prison

is" (III, 1334), reverses the idea of death as a democrat, making him a "Despot" and a "King", but, oddly enough, makes him a rather kindly autocrat. Though the coffin is a prison and the tomb a dungeon, the prison is "soft" and the bars are "sweet", and rest is possible here: "No Despot but the King of Down/ Invented this Repose".

Even if death be all, and there be no immortality, need one despair? The final stanza suggests the answer:

> Of Fate if this is All
> Has he no added Realm
> A dungeon but a Kinsman is
> Incarceration—Home.

If fate has no other realm, if the grave is the end, the prospect is still not too grim. One may look upon this "soft" prison as a place of rest, a secure "Home" where repose is possible. The "Despot", the "King of Down", is a benevolent ruler—a father anxious only that his children not be disturbed.

In "Death is the supple Suitor" (III, 1445), death has the character of a skillful lover wooing a maid. There is no doubt of his ultimate success, of course, and yet death moves with slow craft, not wishing to offend by being too bold:

> It is a stealthy Wooing
> Conducted first
> By pallid innuendoes
> And dim approach

After insinuating himself into the good graces of the

"maid", he then moves with the dash and abandon of a cavalier, coming with bugles and a coach, and

> It bears away in triumph
> To Troth unknown
> And Kinsmen as divulgeless
> As throngs of Down—

The imagery is consistent throughout, beginning with the *suitor* conducting his *wooing* and finally carrying the maid off in his coach to plight their *troth* and meet his *kinsmen*.

Here is a complete picture of death as seen through the eyes of an honest observer who has been able to follow death's wooing up to a point, but no further. One can observe his approach, but once he has carried away the object of his pursuit he is beyond observation, gone "To Troth unknown/ And Kinsmen as divulgeless/ As throngs of Down". What happens after death's departure is only conjecture. The "Kinsmen" will not divulge the secret, for they are members of the same clan as the "King of Down" and are as silent as sleep.

In her last poem personifying death, "Apparently with no surprise" (III, 1624), written about 1884, Emily Dickinson places the blame for death directly upon God. Here, she again symbolizes death by the familiar image of frost and personifies him as the "blonde Assassin". The frost acts as a headsman:

> Apparently with no surprise
> To any happy Flower
> The Frost beheads it at it's play—
> In accidental power—

The blonde Assassin passes on—
The Sun proceeds unmoved
To measure off another Day
For an Approving God.

Throughout her life Emily Dickinson's intense interest in death never abated. Yet the very intensity of her concentration on death, along with the fact that she was never firmly convinced of immortality or of the purpose of death in the world, could cause her to shift the burden, by way of relief, to God. In a mood of despair she wonders if she is the only thing in the universe disturbed about death. The flower itself is not surprised; death is casual, the sun is unmoved, and God must approve since he is omnipotent. Here again is that separation which is so pronounced in her poetry. Nature's attitude toward death is *not* the same as man's. The complacency of sun and flower in the face of death differs sharply from her own intense concern. This pronounced sense of alienation and isolation from the natural order suggests her existential orientation.

After 1865 Emily Dickinson devoted herself increasingly to the composition of elegies. Some, as earlier in her life, she apparently wrote for imaginary people—at least the people are not identified. Most of her later elegies were written for particular occasions, however, and many were sent to friends as messages of consolation. Personally absorbed though she was with her study of death, Emily Dickinson recognized that death was not her exclusive property. Indeed, her own efforts to deal effectively with death made her all the more responsive to the grief of others who had lost close friends or relatives.

One should not, however, lose sight of the fact that, while she sent these poems with the sincere desire to relieve sorrow, she also wrote them to relieve her own concern about death. Poems in this fourth category served as one of her ways of verbally testing her ideas on death.

"So proud she was to die" (III, 1272), written about 1873, concerns an unknown person. The poem pays tribute to one who accepts death and dies bravely, but also voices Dickinson's familiar personal emotion aroused by death—jealousy. The living grow ashamed "That what we cherished, so unknown/ To her desire seemed". What they "cherished" was not only the life of the dying girl, but life in general, which the girl had willingly relinquished and was therefore "unknown to her desire". She was, in fact,

> So satisfied to go
> Where none of us should be
> Immediately—that Anguish stooped
> Almost to Jealousy—

Mourning and anguish over the death turn into jealousy. Knowing Emily Dickinson's eager desire for knowledge of what happens after death, one understands the motive for the "jealousy". The poet was truly envious of one who now was to "walk within the riddle".

Emily Dickinson wrote several tributes in memory of

her father, who died June 16, 1874. For Emily, he had
been the living symbol of rectitude and the Puritan
past, and she reacted to him much as she did to Puritanism—with respect, fear, awe, ridicule, resentment. But
there can be little question that she felt great dependence on her father and that his death was a great blow.
The final impression he left on his daughter, judging
from the elegies in his memory, was that of great
strength and an undeviating sense of virtue.

These four lines, written about 1874, were very likely
in memory of him:

> From his slim Palace in the Dust
> He relegates the Realm,
> More loyal for the exody
> That has befallen him.   (III, 1300)

The imagery in this poem supports the view that Edward Dickinson was indeed the "ruler" of his family.
Palace, Realm, loyal—in no uncertain terms these words
give the impression of a king and his subjects. From his
"Palace" in the ground, he now relegates his kingdom
to his subordinates, loyal to him in his absence. Even in
death, Edward Dickinson continues to extend control
over his family. He may wish to relegate his "Realm",
but his subjects still consider him king.

Another four-line tribute, written about 1874, pictures her father as a strong cedar, felled by an undeserved blow:

> To break so vast a Heart
> Required a Blow as vast—

> No Zephyr felled this Cedar straight—
> 'Twas undeserved Blast—   (III, 1312)

Among other things to Emily Dickinson, her father was the symbol of great strength. To destroy such power required a superhuman force. No soft, gentle breeze could fell such a tree. Only a violent, unexpected gust of wind could destroy the cedar. *Blast* also conveys the idea of something noxious and evil, as a blight. Death is a blast and is a force of evil in the world. As long as one remains uncertain of the purpose of death, and uncertain of what follows, death must be considered *undeserved*. Although Emily Dickinson was thinking of her father when she wrote this poem, she also gave expression to her general views on death.

In January, 1876, Emily wrote to T. W. Higginson a letter which included these words: "Mr. Bowles lent me flowers twice, for my Father's Grave" (II, 547). Following this remark was a four-line poem:

> To his simplicity
> To die—was little Fate—
> If Duty live—contented
> But her Confederate.   (III, 1352)

This sense of duty is the aspect of Edward Dickinson's character which remained longest in his daughter's memory. Not only did he uphold the Puritan traditions of Amherst's past, but he had accepted the orthodox Congregationalism of his day. His secure religious faith and Puritan "simplicity" enabled him to die unafraid: "To die—was little Fate". Since Edward Dickinson felt he had been "saved", to die would hold no terror. Yet if it were his duty to live, he would also be contented. The uprightness of his will, his strict devotion to the "right", permitted him to accept life or death equally— he was content as long as he was duty's confederate. It is the upright will which Emily remembers.

Shortly after the death of his wife in 1878, Emily sent a poem of consolation to T. W. Higginson. She first wrote Higginson in April, 1862, asking for criticism of some enclosed poems. While she changed not a single poem to suit his suggestions, she referred to Higginson as her "tutor" and signed many of her letters, "Your Scholar". Though Higginson talked with her in person only twice, in 1870 and 1873,[9] the two corresponded for over twenty years and seemed to have a genuinely high regard for each other. She continued to enclose poems from time to time, and apparently he continued to comment upon them. In a way, Higginson served as an audience for her poetry and filled, perhaps, the need she might have felt for some literary figure at least to see her poems.

The poem sent to him after the death of his wife begins, "How brittle are the Piers/ On which our Faith doth tread" (III, 1433). With exceptionally good taste she seems to have sensed what Higginson's feelings must have been at this time. She recognizes that the "Piers" of his faith must surely be tottering after such a loss. Yet perhaps he will take comfort knowing that he is not alone on this shaky bridge: "none hath such a Crowd".

Higginson at one time had been a Unitarian minister,

and though he liked to consider himself a "liberal" and a "radical", he was in many ways conventional—minded. Emily Dickinson felt that at such a time he might be happy to resort to the crutch of Christianity, and in the concluding stanza of the elegy she tries to assure him that this "tottering bridge" is not so weak as it appears: "It is as old as God", and was in fact "built by him—/ He sent his Son to test the Plank,/ And he pronounced it firm".

The Reverend Charles Wadsworth, the Presbyterian minister whom Emily called her "dearest earthly friend", died in April, 1882. Later in the year she included a four–line poem in a letter to James D. Clark, who had been a friend of the minister. The poem is in memory of Wadsworth:

> Obtaining but our own Extent
> In whatsoever Realm—
> 'Twas Christ's own personal Expanse
> That bore him from the Tomb— (III, 1543)

A high tribute, the implication is that Wadsworth, like Christ, will achieve immortality by dint of his faultless character. Wherever Wadsworth may be, that realm will be heaven; his own strong will and personal force will determine his environment, even the environment of immortality. The poem also shows the influence of Transcendentalism in the idea of the self–sufficiency of the individual. Each man, capable of realizing the highest ideals, must himself recognize his potentialities and act to fulfill them. Each is capable of unlimited "personal Expanse".

Occasionally Emily Dickinson would let a single poem apply to more than one person. Such is the case with the poem beginning "Pass to thy Rendezvous of Light" (III, 1564). There are two manuscripts, identical in text except for the omission of a dash in the second line of one version. Emily Dickinson's eight–year–old nephew Gilbert, son of Austin and Susan Dickinson, died in October, 1883, and Emily included the poem in a note to Susan sent shortly after Gilbert's death. In February, 1885, she sent the lines in a letter to Higginson. One of her favorite women authors was George Eliot, and Emily sent as a gift to Higginson a copy of J. W. Cross's *George Eliot's Life*.[10] The poem in this case applies to George Eliot. The four lines read:

> Pass to thy Rendezvous of Light,
> Pangless except for us—
> Who slowly ford the Mystery
> Which thou hast leaped across!

Though written as a tribute to the memory of her nephew and to George Eliot, the poem allowed Emily Dickinson to express one of her familiar views on death. The dead suffer no pangs; it is the living who feel the pain—pain, of course, from genuine regret that the dead will no longer be present, but also pain from another source—jealousy. Emily Dickinson's intense anticipation and anxiety of what lay beyond death, her eagerness to resolve her doubts, to face whatever it was that occurred after the physical demise of the body, gave rise to envy of those who had been admitted to the mystery.

The dead knew whether there was any "purple flower" across the brook. It was the slow fording of the stream, the tension of anticipation that gave the pangs.

Emily Dickinson was extremely fond of children, and apparently the relationship between young Gilbert and his aunt was very close. She sent the following four–line poem to Susan when Gilbert died in 1883:

> Climbing to reach the costly Hearts
> To which he gave the worth,
> He broke them, fearing punishment
> He ran away from Earth—   (III, 1566)

By all accounts, Gilbert was an unusually personable and likeable child, and there were further reasons for his being especially dear to the Dickinson family. He was born to Austin and Susan after they had been married almost twenty years and, perhaps most important, was born in the year following Edward Dickinson's death. Gilbert's presence doubtless aided the family in turning their attention away from the death of the father. For these reasons, Gilbert's death eight years later was especially sorrowful.[11]

The poem contains terms particularly associated with childhood—*climbing, punishment, ran away*—and, because of these terms, is effective and appropriate. The poem is sentimental, but it is not maudlin. Coming from an aunt exceedingly fond of her nephew, it shows, in fact, remarkable restraint. Unquestionably the child did give much of "the worth" to the "Hearts" of the adults in his family. Emily could not be clinical in writing these lines. She does not here objectively test any general ideas on death and immortality. She was too close to the child and could not be analytical.

Emily Dickinson wrote at least one elegy in memory of her mother, who died in November, 1882. Emily's letters give no adequate portrait of her mother, for references to Mrs. Dickinson are relatively few. Apparently she was rather overshadowed and subordinated by the personality of Edward Dickinson. Her major function, it appears, was to be a dutiful wife and to keep charge of household affairs. The relationship between mother and daughter was not close and they seem to have had little in common.[12] The remark Emily made to T. W. Higginson is revealing: "My Mother does not care for thought" (II, 404).

Mrs. Dickinson was paralyzed about a year after her husband's death. From that time until her death in November, 1882, the responsibility for the care of her mother fell largely upon Emily, and the two unavoidably became closer than they had ever been. Apparently Emily changed her attitude toward her mother during this time, for she wrote to her Norcross cousins shortly after Mrs. Dickinson's death that:

> She was scarcely the aunt you knew. The great mission of pain had been ratified—cultivated to tenderness by persistent sorrow, so that a larger mother died than had she died before.   (III, 750)

In a letter to her friend Maria Whitney, Emily incorporated a poem written in memory of her mother.

It is the one beginning, "To the bright east she flies"
(III, 1573). The first stanza, somewhat puzzling, becomes clear only in the light of biographical information. The stanza states that paradise will

> Remit her home,
> Without a change of wings,
> Or Love's convenient things,
> Enticed to come.

Despite the fact that Mrs. Dickinson had been an invalid for several years, her actual death seemed very sudden. Emily wrote her cousins: "I hoped to write you
before, but mother's dying almost stunned my spirit. . . .
There was no earthly parting. She slipped from our
fingers like a flake gathered by the wind" (III, 749–50).
Her mother was "Enticed to come" suddenly and with
no warning, no time for "a change of wings". Members
of her family, having no warning, could not give her
any final words of comfort, any of "Love's convenient
things".

The second stanza applies no longer to the mother
but to the ones thinking of her death:

> Fashioning what she is,
> Fathoming what she was,
> We deem we dream—
> And that dissolves the days
> Through which existence strays
> Homeless at home.

In the line "Fashioning what she is", Emily Dickinson
again conveys her thoughts on immortality by her

choice of a particular word. The mother is dead, and "what she is" now, the poet can only imagine. Having no positive assurance of what happens after death, the daughter can only contrive, or form, or *fashion* some notion of "what she is".

"Fathoming what she was" refers to Emily's own recently gained insight into her mother's character, the knowledge that "a larger mother died than had she died before".

The rest of the poem conveys a feeling of numbness left by the aftermath of death. Trying to "fashion" an idea of immortality and trying to "fathom" what her mother was fill the days. The shock of death produces a dream–like state that "dissolves the days". The verb *strays*, conveying the feeling of aimlessness and lack of direction, is in keeping with the mood started by the verb *dream*. The poet is wandering or *straying*, as in a dream, and indicates the acuteness of her sense of loss by the final line "Homeless at home". In many ways Emily Dickinson's home was her world, and after the death of her father she rarely left its immediate vicinity. From one so strongly attached to home and so dependent upon it, the words "Homeless at home" clearly express an acute sense of hopelessness and loss.

Emily Dickinson wrote many other commemorative verses in memory of friends who were important in her life. To such people as Samuel Bowles, Dr. J. G. Holland, Judge Otis P. Lord, and Helen Hunt Jackson, she paid tribute in poetry, producing some of her better elegies. The elegies discussed in this chapter, however, have been selected not so much for their merits as tributes to the dead as for what they reveal of Emily Dickinson's attitude toward death.

The poems from the final period reveal that Emily Dickinson never abandoned her determined efforts to understand death, though the intensity and urgent fascination of her interest, so prominent in the poems of the middle period, seem to have diminished. In many instances the poems in this final group assume a somewhat puzzling quality, the result of a rather odd blending of resentment and stoic acceptance—resentment against her own exhausting religious quest for knowledge of death, and stoic acceptance of the fact of death—an acceptance that may have been caused by the depletion of her strength and energy and from her growing awareness that no answers would be forthcoming in this world.

The Role of Death in Emily Dickinson's Poetry

❖

EMILY DICKINSON'S EXISTENTIAL AWARE-ness of the reality and the "problem" of death had a pervasive influence on the content of the poems she wrote and, indeed, was the principal reason for her turning her energies to poetic composition of any kind. As she put it, in a letter to T. W. Higginson: "I sing, as the Boy does by the Burying Ground—because I am afraid" (II, 404)—afraid, that is, of death. The remark to her Norcross cousins that she "sang off charnel steps" (II, 436) is a further indication that the poet herself knew that death, and more particularly a fear of it, was a prime motivating force in her creative work. To occupy her mind and to reduce her anxiety over death, she turned to a "study" of the dictionary. She told Higginson that after the death of one of her early "tutors", probably Benjamin Newton, "for several years, my Lexicon—was my only companion" (II, 404). This interest in words must have helped give rise to her early efforts to write poetry.

What originally turned Emily Dickinson's attention to death? The religious nature of her environment focused her attention on death and immortality. The town in which she lived was still very definitely attached to its Puritan traditions. Though her father did not join the church until rather late in life, he was from "the old school of Puritanism", and there is no question but that his daughter was reared in an atmosphere of earnest Christian thinking.[1] From all sides she felt a pressure to experience "conversion". Even in the nineteenth century, the heritage of Calvinism was very much alive in Amherst.

Emily Dickinson's inability to experience a personal conversion resulted in doubt and apprehension, especially when she was at the South Hadley Female Seminary (Mount Holyoke). Witnessing the conversion of her classmates, seeing how eagerly they sought the "message", she became increasingly aware that she was among the "lost" and was "one of the lingering bad ones". Would death without conversion close the gates to heaven? She was unsure of heaven, while her contemporaries who had been "saved" claimed to have absolute certainty of its existence. In his *English Notebooks*, Nathaniel Hawthorne said of his friend Herman Melville: "He can neither believe, nor be comfortable in his unbelief; and he is too honest and courageous not to try to do one or the other". Emily Dickinson, too, wavered between doubt and belief all of her life and, like Melville, was too courageous to give up her honest pursuit of truth. She expressed her paradoxical position in the lines:

> Of Paradise' existence
> All we know
> Is the uncertain certainty—   (III, 1411)

For a moment she saw a way out of her religious diffi-
culties. If, as Emerson asserted, all men were potentially
divine, then there would be no such thing as a membership of the "elect", arbitrarily chosen by God, and she
would not be abandoned among the "lost". Furthermore, according to the Transcendentalists, the individual should trust himself rather than tradition. Emily
eagerly responded. She would gladly trust her own insight and intuition as against the word of authority. To
do so might relieve her from the haunting fear that she
was not one of God's chosen.

Puritanism was too much a part of her, however, for
the gospel of Transcendentalism to win her total allegiance. Though attracted to the optimistic assertions of
Transcendentalism, she continued to see man's position
in the universe as an insecure one. Was not death ready
to strike at any moment? What if, after all, God *did* receive only the "saved"? Better that one should be constantly alert—better that the door be left slightly ajar
to allow God's light, if it should come, to enter. Her
lack of total commitment to either view led to spiritual
unrest, while her direct observation of death "in action"
gave support to neither. And it was this direct, raw,
"naive" experience, this personal discovery, that links
her attitude with that of existentialism. She was an individual who existed *in time*, intensely aware of the
menace of death in every moment. This cold, still, silent thing—the corpse—looked no more like a member

of the "elect" than it looked like a self–sufficient private man. Was man infinite or dependent? Should he move with caution or with bold optimism? On these questions Emily Dickinson was unfortunately in the middle, pulled from both directions, throughout her adult life:

> Go slow, my soul, to feed thyself
> Upon his rare approach—
> Go rapid, lest Competing Death
> Prevail upon the Coach—
> Go timid, lest his final eye
> Determine thee amiss—
> Go boldly—for thou paid'st his price
> Redemption—for a Kiss—   (III, 1297)

With the coming of the Civil War, the reality of death prompted her to the fullest use of her poetic talents. She wrote poetry to relieve her anxieties, gazing at death from all sides, testing her vision within the context of her poems, hoping to get close to death, hoping to cope with it artistically. She was not attempting to prove anything; she was not preaching a gospel or trying to present a consistent theory about death. Though she may have hoped that one day her poems might be widely read, she did not write them for this purpose. She wrote them for herself, as a release from emotional stress.

In her poems of death and immortality and in her elegies she gives her ideas free play. They are not consistent. She expresses hope for immortality, then doubt. She pictures this life as merely a test for the next, then as all. She praises God, then condemns Him. She sees man as divine, then as lowly.

In her poems treating the physical aspects of death

she makes certain observations from the viewpoint of sensations, finding the most persistent qualities of the dead to be coldness, immobility, weight, and silence.

Her poems personifying death find "him" to have as many contradictions as the universe, and as many complexities. He is timid and bold. He is a lover, a murderer, a brigand, a thoughtful coachman, a democrat, a despot, a comforter, a wild beast. She has no final view of death personified. He remains the great unknown, the great mystery.

Emily Dickinson's poetry also served as a substitute for religion. Very definitely wanting to have a firm religious belief, she could not honestly accept the religion of her time. After their father's death she wrote her Norcross cousins in January, 1863: "Let Emily sing for you because she cannot pray" (II, 421). Here is a distinct indication that she wrote poetry, that she "sang", because she could not pray in the conventional manner to a God whose grace she had not received.

In her best poems Emily Dickinson expressed her fears and oppositions, the conflicts born of Puritan doubts and Transcendental hopes, by images drawn from everyday experience and personal observation. Not an abstract thinker or philosopher, she pulled the abstract down into the world of specific sensation where she could turn, touch, weigh, and handle these concepts.

Death as an awesome force in the universe, thoughts not subject to the test of observation and experience she views existentially through the concrete and homely images of the house: freckled pane, cobweb, buzzing fly, indolent housewife, sweeping, early task, bustle in the house, spools of thread, busy needles, stirring house. In similar fashion she used images familiar to her from her interest in flowers and plants: husk, kernel, pod, sod, crocus, sprig, roses. Observation of nature in her garden led her to associate death with frost and snow—thus, the many *cold* images in connection with death. Her firsthand observations of deaths in neighboring houses, observations made in the presence of the dying, observations of the gear and ceremonies connected with burials and funerals lent further concrete substance to her poems. The undertaker is the "man of the appalling trade". Death "Dresses each House in Crape, and Icicle". Death takes a friend; those present in the room "placed the Hair and drew the Head erect", and the body now appeared "Too stiff to bended be".

Her attitude toward death influenced Emily Dickinson's technique—the actual combination of words as they appear in the poems. Her basic metrical pattern was that of the hymn books, but with variations. Even here, one can see the influence of her inner conflicts over death and her doubts of immortality. In one sense, at least, her poetry was a great effort to understand death, God, and immortality—a great prayer or hymn for the resolution of her doubts. The external form that she chose, the hymn, reflects her attitude toward her subject matter—a desire to relieve her fear and anxious concern over death and immortality. Unable to join a church, she could offer her own unorthodox "hymns" in an effort to catch God's ear.

While Emily Dickinson's irregularities in rhyme were primarily a device to allow her greater freedom in choice of words, attitude and mood also influenced her use of approximate rhyme. She apparently followed no rule in using approximate rhyme in one place, exact rhyme in another. She did *not* use approximate rhyme only in those poems expressing the fractured nature of the universe. And she did *not* use exact rhyme only in her "light" verse or in poems expressing affirmation or optimistic hope. She did *not* picture the universe, or even the world, as neatly divided into black and white, evil or good, discord or harmony, false rhyme or true rhyme. Here was another point, of course, at which she was at variance with the "saved" and "damned" mentality of Puritanism. To her the world was not this simple. It was a highly intricate and puzzling melange, a mixing of good and evil, of exact rhyme and false rhyme. The very fact that she used a mixture of true rhyme and approximate rhyme reflects her feeling that the universe is an aggregate of elements, arranged—if, indeed, they are arranged—in no simple either–or fashion.

Her attitude toward death influenced certain other characteristics of her verse. The sense of urgency and haste running throughout her poetry reflects her acute awareness of the presence of death, ready at any moment to cut life short. As she told T. W. Higginson, "Shortness to live has made me bold", and she wrote:

Why should we hurry—why indeed
When every way we fly
We are molested equally
by immortality   (III, 1646)

Even her use of the dash reflects—and conveys—a feeling of haste and urgency. Impatient with punctuation,
afraid to slow down her creative thought, she placed a
dash wherever she desired. In similar fashion she
omitted auxiliary verbs, brushing them aside boldly
to hasten her conclusion.[2] Her fondness for the subjunctive, too, seems to be in keeping with her persistent
attitude of doubt.

But her technique involved more than the use of
hymn meters, approximate rhyme, eccentricities in the
use of the dash, fondness for the subjunctive, and omission of auxiliaries. The heart of her technique, whether
planned or instinctive, was her selection and arrangement of words in a poetic structure. An intense interest
in words as such was central to her poetics. Her ability
to let words mold and shape each other in context, the
interplay of the various connotations of her words, their
interaction on one another—here is the core of her
"style".

Her attitude toward death influenced this last aspect
of her technique, for *if* she could use words in unconventional ways, *if* she could unite the like with the
unlike by sudden and unexpected juxtapositions, *if* she
could consider the complexities and contradictions of
words and unite them into an artistic whole in her
poem—then perhaps she could accept the incongruities

in the universe. If she could join into a meaningful whole seemingly disparate words, then perhaps she could entertain the notion that an apparently disordered universe might in reality be intact, though she would not be admitted to the secret in this life.

Emily Dickinson was ever conscious of "Death's tremendous nearness". The sound of death was rarely beyond hearing distance. Though she never resolved her conflicts, in a sense she triumphed over death by transmuting the uncertainties of her experience into the art of her poetry.[3]

There can be little question that death was her central theme. Clearly it colored all her thinking and gave its tint to the majority of her poems. Even in her lighter verse, death slyly peeks out, largely hidden but none the less there. To call this concern "morbid", as some have done, is to miss the point.[4] For Emily Dickinson, death was the one unmistakable, though undefinable, force in an equivocal universe. Punctual, reliable, dependable, inevitable, absolute—it was the one certainty in a world of uncertainties. A totally independent power, it emerged as the focal point in her thought, her central subject of inquiry. It rose above all else—supreme, omnipresent, and omnipotent. Little wonder that death became, in effect, her "poetic principle". Though not a philosopher, she poetically pursued her interest with Yankee tenacity.

Was the end worth the pursuit? Her poems are the answer.

Notes

❖

CHAPTER I

1. George F. Whicher, *This Was a Poet* (New York, 1938), p. 298; Richard Chase, *Emily Dickinson* (New York, 1951), p. 230; Thomas H. Johnson, *Emily Dickinson: An Interpretive Biography* (Cambridge, 1955), p. 203; Charles R. Anderson, *Emily Dickinson's Poetry: Stairway of Surprise* (New York, 1960), p. 284. I am greatly indebted to these major studies of Emily Dickinson. I should indicate, however, how my approach to the poet differs in several important respects.

I have emphasized death as the principal controlling factor in Emily Dickinson's thought and poetry from the beginning to the end of her creative life, whereas Chase, Whicher, Johnson, and Anderson consider death as but *one* significant factor in her development, and as perhaps the final stage in that development. For example, Johnson and Anderson each devote but a single chapter to death—in each case the one next to the last, immediately preceding a final chapter on immortality. In each book death is the "White Exploit". Johnson considers death as one of her "Flood Subjects", while in Anderson's book death appears as the important factor in the last of a four–part arrangement leading from Emily Dickinson's theory of art, to the "Outer World", to the "Inner World", and finally to the "Other Paradise"—which includes death.

The most significant difference, however, between Anderson's treatment of death and my own is that whereas Anderson finds "no marked periods in her career, no significant curve of development in her artistic powers", my study theorizes that there were distinct periods of development, each with its recognizable characteristics.

Whicher, though recognizing the importance of death to the poet, treats the subject almost as an afterthought in a few pages near the end of his book.

Chase very definitely recognizes death as her prevailing subject, and the author is indebted to him. However, though he does refer to death at intervals throughout his book, he devotes only seven or eight pages near the end of his volume to a specific treatment of her poems on death.

For the views of other critics who are aware of Emily Dickinson's concern with death, see the following articles:

Conrad Aiken, "Emily Dickinson", *Dial*, LXXVI (April, 1924), 301-308. Aiken was one of the first critics to point to the fact that Emily Dickinson had written a remarkably large number of poems on death, and to aver that her genius was fully at work in these poems. However, I disagree emphatically with his contention that ultimately the "obsession became morbid".

John Crowe Ransom, "Emily Dickinson: A Poet Restored", *Perspectives U S A*, No. 15 (Spring, 1956), pp. 5–20. This article begins with a discussion of two of Emily Dickinson's death poems.

Austin Warren, "Emily Dickinson", *Sewanee Review*, LXV (Autumn, 1957), pp. 565–86. Warren's article ends with a brief discussion of Emily Dickinson's death poems and the comment that they are "probably the best poems Emily ever wrote".

Louise Bogan, "A Mystical Poet", *Emily Dickinson: Three Views* (Amherst, 1960), pp. 27–34. I must emphatically take issue with this critic's contention that Emily Dickinson's favorite subject was not death. The evidence does not support her assertion that the poet moved away from "her early slight addiction to graveyardism".

Archibald MacLeish, "The Private World: Poems of Emily Dickinson", *Poetry and Experience* (Boston, 1960), pp. 91–114. MacLeish shows a keen awareness of the importance of our topic when he states that "death is, of course, her familiar theme".

2. Martha Dickinson Bianchi, *The Life and Letters of Emily Dickinson* (Boston and New York, 1924), p. 83.

3. Mable Loomis Todd and Millicent Todd Bingham (eds.), *Bolts of Melody* (New York and London, 1945), p. 5.

4. Letters quoted or mentioned in this study are to be found in *The Letters of Emily Dickinson,* ed. by Thomas H. Johnson and Theodora Ward (Cambridge, 1958). The roman numerals in parentheses indicate volume numbers, the arabic numerals page numbers.

5. Anderson sees the poetry as essentially "religious" in Paul Tillich's sense of "asking passionately the question of the meaning of our existence" (pp. 283–84).

6. Johnson sees her poems as not only a relief from apprehensions, but also a means of "being richly alive" (p. 205).

7. Anderson suggests that "loss in the grave raising the

hope of reunion in heaven, is probably the oldest motivation to a belief in immortality" (p. 225).

8. The poems quoted or mentioned in this study may all be found in *The Poems of Emily Dickinson*, ed. by Thomas H. Johnson (Cambridge, 1955). The roman numerals in parentheses indicate volume numbers, the arabic numerals poem numbers.

9. Anderson recognizes her "tension between faith and doubt", a state of mind that remained "constant from an early age down to her death" (p. 257).

10. *Ibid.*, p. 285. Anderson believes that "alternating doubt and belief held her mind unresolved to the very end".

11. Richard Chase seems to agree that Emily Dickinson's doubts about immortality remained with her, but maintains that "it is understood between man and God that this painful cat-and-mouse game . . . is to end with the final disbursement of God's wealth: immortality" (p. 180)—a reading with which I am not in accord.

12. Anderson sees this use of "domestic imagery" in dealing with death as her "unique strategy" (p. 230).

13. That Emily Dickinson was not a systematic thinker is pointed out by Anderson, p. 285; Chase, p. 131; Whicher, pp. 162, 291, 305.

14. Emily Dickinson nearly always misspelled the possessive of *it* as *it's*. Henceforth this irregularity will not be indicated by *sic*. In all quotations the apostrophe appears exactly as Emily Dickinson used it.

15. Theodore Spencer, *Death and Elizabethan Tragedy* (Cambridge, 1936), p. 69.

16. *Ibid.*, p. 76.

17. *Ibid.*, p. 83.

18. *Ibid.*, p. 90.

19. Leonard P. Kurtz, *The Dance of Death and the Macabre Spirit in European Literature* (New York, 1934), p. 259.

20. *Ibid.*, p. 226.

21. Spencer, p. 84.

22. *Ibid.*, p. 156.

23. Whicher, p. 224.

24. Johnson, p. 81.

25. *Ibid.*, p. 205.

26. *Ibid.*, p. 203.

27. For the importance of this subject to Emily Dickinson see Anderson, p. 231, and Johnson, p. 207.

28. Anderson, p. 239, sees the poet's use of her writings as a means of knowing death, since the "traditional decorum for facing death had proved inadequate to her".

29. Johnson comments on the variety of her attitudes toward death (p. 203).

30. See note 13 above. Johnson sees somewhat more system in her thought, saying that "she worked out a philosophic testament" (p. 232), and that she "wrote a whole series of poems that establish her philosophical position on the nature and destiny of man" (p. 240).

31. Allen Tate and George Frisbie Whicher, among others, have noted this use of the abstract joined with the concrete. Tate, in his essay "Emily Dickinson" in *Reactionary Essays on Poetry and Ideas* (New York, 1936), points out how she sets up a tension between abstraction and sensation. Whicher finds many "examples of the immaterial stated with startling elaboration in terms of the material". He also recognizes that the "identification of seemingly unlike things was her constant habit" (p. 296).

CHAPTER II

1. Johnson, *Emily Dickinson*: *An Interpretive Biography*, p. 8. I am indebted to Johnson's graphic discussion of the Puritan background of Amherst. It may be well to note at the outset that the purpose of this chapter is to show the special relevance of certain well–known biographical facts to the theme of death in Dickinson's poetry. Nothing new or startling is offered by way of biographical detail, as such.

2. *Ibid.*, p. 11.

3. *Ibid.*, pp. 16–18.

4. Ralph Barton Perry, *Puritanism and Democracy* (New York, 1944), p. 219.

5. *Ibid.*, p. 225.

6. *Ibid.*, p. 93.

7. Johnson, p. 11.

8. William Dean Howells, "The Strange Poems of Emily Dickinson", *Harper's Magazine*, LXXXII (January, 1891), p. 318.

9. *Ibid.*, pp. 319–20.

10. Johnson, pp. 17–18.

11. Perry, p. 86.

12. Thomas W. Higginson, "Emily Dickinson's Letters", *Atlantic Monthly*, LXVIII (October, 1891), p. 452.

13. *Ibid.*

14. See Johnson, pp. 24–32, for an excellent portrait of Emily Dickinson's father; also see Whicher, pp. 24–28.

15. Millicent Todd Bingham, *Emily Dickinson's Home* (New York, 1955), p. xi.

16. *Ibid.*, p. 100.

17. *Ibid.*, p. 33.

18. For the material about Mount Holyoke, I am especially indebted to George Frisbie Whicher, *This Was a Poet*, pp. 58–76; for other perceptive discussions see Johnson, pp. 12–16, and Richard Chase, *Emily Dickinson*, pp. 50–57.

19. Whicher, p. 59.

20. Johnson, p. 13.

21. Whicher, pp. 191–92.

22. *Ibid.*, p. 194.

23. *Ibid.*

24. *Ibid.*, p. 89. Whicher writes that "there were few people in Amherst then who did not regard him askance".

25. I am indebted to Johnson, pp. 233–34, for his comments on the effects of Puritanism and Transcendentalism.

26. See Whicher's chapter on "Emerson" in *This Was a Poet* for an enlightening discussion. I disagree, however, with his contention that Emersonian ideas "may be detected in Emily Dickinson's poems as easily as in Whitman's, but it is not profitable to single them out" (p. 198). I feel that specific resemblances offer the best evidence of kinship, regardless of whether that kinship is strictly to Emerson himself or to Emerson as a representative of the times.

27. Howells, "The Strange Poems of Emily Dickinson", *loc. cit.*, 319.

28. Bingham, p. 176.

29. *Ibid.*, p. 178.

30. *Ibid.*, pp. 179–80.

31. Johnson, p. 205.

32. Bingham, p. 170.

33. Anderson, *Emily Dickinson's Poetry*, p. 239.

34. There is really no term that is quite so apt as "clini-

cal", used by both Whicher and Johnson in describing her impersonal attitude. See Whicher, p. 162; and Johnson, p. 203.

CHAPTER III

1. Johnson, *Emily Dickinson: An Interpretive Biography*, p. 85, and Whicher, *This Was a Poet*, p. 240. The purpose of this chapter is to relate Dickinson's prosody and idiosyncrasies in grammar and syntax to her treatment of the theme of death, rather than to present a full review of her experiments in prosody and eccentric syntax in general, such as can be found in Johnson's and Whicher's studies.

2. For perceptive accounts of Emily Dickinson's metrical patterns see Whicher, pp. 240–43, and Johnson, pp. 84–92.

3. See Whicher, pp. 243–49, for a full account of Emily Dickinson's use of rhyme.

4. For rewarding accounts of her eccentricities in grammar and language, see Whicher, pp. 231–36, and Johnson, pp. 92–94.

5. The author is indebted to Whicher's discussion in *This Was a Poet*, pp. 247–48. Johnson, however, sees her uncertainty reflected in the metric fluctuation of "There's a certain Slant of light" (p. 190).

6. Johnson and Anderson seem to be at odds on this point. Whereas Johnson sees a "marked change" occurring in the "nature and virtuosity of the poems" after 1865, Anderson insists that there are "no marked periods in her career". (See Johnson, p. 239; Anderson, p. xii). The present study supports the thesis that there *were* definite periods in her development.

7. Johnson (ed.), *The Poems of Emily Dickinson* (III, 1200–1201).

8. Johnson, p. 207, characterizes her earliest poems as "sentimentally funereal".

9. Anderson, p. xiv.

CHAPTER IV

1. Richard Chase makes some interesting observations on Emily Dickinson's interest in words. In *Emily Dickinson* he says that her "faith in the efficacy of words, in a kind of word magic, is one of the permanent acquisitions of the period we are considering" (p. 107), adding that her "cultivation of language is, to be sure, her strength as well as her weakness" (p. 200).

2. Whereas the present study sets up "death and immortality" as *one* of four groups which comprise Emily Dickinson's poems on death, showing how poems in this particular group reveal the intimate relation she saw between death and immortality, Johnson in *Emily Dickinson: An Interpretive Biography*, sees death and immortality as "two distinct subjects" (p. 232).

3. Johnson points to this characteristic when he writes that the "search . . . is in fact being made by the poet who, in the presence of death, hopes to find an answer to the riddle of death" (p. 209).

4. This group is very similar to the one that Johnson names as the first of his three groups (p. 203). Chase implies a similar category when he speaks of "New England deathbed scenes and funerals" (p. 246).

5. Johnson, p. 204.

6. Chase, p. 233.

7. Both Whicher, pp. 180–81, and Chase, p. 198, point

to this marked characteristic of expressing the "spiritual" in terms of the "ordinary".

8. Johnson sees personification of death as one of three groups of death poems, and discusses this use on pp. 218–24 of his biography. Also see Chase, p. 233.

9. Chase, p. 175.

10. *Ibid.*, p. 106. Chase notes her use of abstract words as if they were concrete.

11. Johnson, p. 230.

12. Chase, p. 130.

CHAPTER V

1. Johnson (ed.), *The Poems of Emily Dickinson* (III, 1201).

2. Both Whicher, *This Was a Poet*, p. 302, and Chase, *Emily Dickinson*, p. 174, call attention to her acute awareness of pain.

3. Anderson, in *Emily Dickinson's Poetry*, maintains that her "best poems on death were not inspired by personal experiences" (p. 227).

4. Higginson, "Emily Dickinson's Letters", *Atlantic Monthly*, LXVIII (October, 1891), p. 453.

5. Johnson (ed.), I, 330.

6. *Ibid.*, II, 457.

CHAPTER VI

1. Johnson, *Emily Dickinson: An Interpretive Biography*, p. 33.

2. *Ibid.*, p. 66. See also Whicher, *This Was a Poet*, pp. 148–49.

3. Todd and Bingham, *Bolts of Melody*, p. 223.

4. Whicher, p. 233.

5. *Ibid.*, p. 292. I am indebted to Whicher for the terms "mind" and "experience", though my use of them differs from his.

6. *Ibid.*, p. 163. Whicher speaks of her "need of a faith".

7. Johnson, pp. 203, 207.

8. Johnson (ed.), *The Poems of Emily Dickinson* (II, 774).

9. Johnson, p. 264.

10. Johnson (ed.), (III, 1078).

11. For a sensitive account of the relation between Emily and Gilbert, see Johnson's biography, pp. 42–44.

12. For discussions of the relationship between Emily and her mother, see Whicher, pp. 28–29, and Johnson, pp. 32–33.

CHAPTER VII

1. Johnson, *Emily Dickinson: An Interpretive Biography*, p. 6.

2. For an account of her "economy" of syntax, see Whicher, *This Was a Poet*, p. 236.

3. Anderson writes in *Emily Dickinson's Poetry* that her poems "enabled her to master death rather than be mastered by it" (p. 239).

4. Anderson is in accord with this idea when he writes that the "natural complement to an intense love of life is an intense fear of death" (p. 228).

A Selected Bibliography

❖

THE POEMS AND LETTERS

Johnson, Thomas H. (ed.) *The Complete Poems of Emily Dickinson.* Boston: Little, Brown & Co., 1960.

Johnson, Thomas H. (ed.) *The Poems of Emily Dickinson.* 3 vols. Cambridge, Mass.: The Belknap Press of Harvard University, 1955.

Johnson, Thomas H., and Ward, Theodora (eds.) *The Letters of Emily Dickinson.* 3 vols. Cambridge, Mass.: The Belknap Press of Harvard University, 1958.

BOOKS ABOUT EMILY DICKINSON

Anderson, Charles R. *Emily Dickinson's Poetry: Stairway of Surprise.* New York: Holt, Rinehart, & Winston, 1960.

Bianchi, Martha Dickinson. *The Life and Letters of Emily Dickinson.* Boston and New York: Houghton Mifflin Co., 1924.

Bingham, Millicent Todd. *Ancestor's Brocades: The Literary Debut of Emily Dickinson.* New York: Harper & Bros., 1945.

Bingham, Millicent Todd. *Emily Dickinson*: *A Revelation*. New York: Harper & Bros., 1954.

Bingham, Millicent Todd. *Emily Dickinson's Home*. New York: Harper & Bros., 1955.

Blake, Caesar R., and Wells, Carlton F. (eds.) *The Recognition of Emily Dickinson*: *Selected Criticism Since 1890*. Ann Arbor: University of Michigan Press, 1964.

Chase, Richard. *Emily Dickinson*. New York: William Sloane Associates, 1951.

Davis, Thomas M. (ed.) *14 By Emily Dickinson*: *With Selected Criticism*. Chicago: Scott, Foresman & Co., 1964.

Gelpi, Albert J. *Emily Dickinson*: *The Mind of the Poet*. Cambridge, Mass.: Harvard University Press, 1965.

Griffith, Clark. *The Long Shadow*: *Emily Dickinson's Tragic Poetry*. Princeton: Princeton University Press, 1964.

Hampson, Alfred Leete. *Emily Dickinson*: *A Bibliography*. Northampton: The Hampshire Bookshop, 1930.

Jenkins, MacGregor. *Emily Dickinson*: *Friend and Neighbor*. Boston: Little, Brown & Co., 1930.

Johnson, Thomas H. *Emily Dickinson*: *An Interpretive Biography*. Cambridge, Mass.: The Belknap Press of Harvard University, 1955.

Jones Library Staff. *Emily Dickinson*: *A Bibliography*. With a Foreword by George Frisbie Whicher. Amherst: The Jones Library, 1930.

Leyda, Jay. *The Years and Hours of Emily Dickinson*. 2 vols. New Haven: Yale University Press, 1960.

Patterson, Rebecca. *The Riddle of Emily Dickinson*. Boston: Houghton Mifflin Co., 1951.

Pollitt, Josephine. *Emily Dickinson*: *The Human Background of Her Poetry*. New York: Harper & Bros., 1930.

Power, Sister Mary James. *In the Name of the Bee*. New York: Sheed & Ward, 1943.

Sewall, Richard B. (ed.) *Emily Dickinson: A Collection of Critical Essays*. Englewood Cliffs: Prentice-Hall, Inc., 1963.

Taggard, Genevieve. *The Life and Mind of Emily Dickinson*. New York: Alfred A. Knopf, Inc., 1930.

Thackrey, Donald E. *Emily Dickinson's Approach to Poetry*. Lincoln: University of Nebraska Press, 1954.

Ward, Theodora. *The Capsule of the Mind: Chapters in the Life of Emily Dickinson*. Cambridge, Mass.: The Belknap Press of Harvard University, 1961.

Wells, Henry W. *Introduction to Emily Dickinson*. Chicago: Packard & Co., 1947.

Whicher, George Frisbie. *This Was a Poet*. New York: Charles Scribner's Sons, 1938.

ARTICLES AND ESSAYS

Aiken, Conrad. "Emily Dickinson", *Dial*, LXXVI (April, 1924), 301–308.

Aldrich, Thomas B. *"In Re* Emily Dickinson", *Atlantic Monthly*, LXIX (January, 1892), 143–144.

Arvin, Newton. "The Poems of Emily Dickinson", *American Literature*, XXVIII (May, 1956), 232–236.

Banzer, Judith. " 'Compound Manner': Emily Dickinson and the Metaphysical Poets", *American Literature*, XXXII (January, 1961), 415–433.

Barbot, Mary E. "Emily Dickinson Parallels", *The New England Quarterly*, XIV (December, 1941), 689–696.

Blackmur, R. P. "Emily Dickinson: Notes on Prejudice

and Fact", *The Expense of Greatness*. New York: Harcourt, Brace & Co., 1952. pp. 25–50.

Bogan, Louise. "A Mystical Poet", *Emily Dickinson: Three Views*. Amherst: Amherst College Press, 1960. pp. 27–34.

Bradford, Gamaliel. "Emily Dickinson", *Atlantic Monthly*, CXXIV (August, 1919), 216–226.

Brown, Rollo Walter. "A Sublimated Puritan", *The Saturday Review of Literature*, V (October 6, 1928), 186–187.

Carpenter, Frederic I. "Emily Dickinson and the Rhymes of Dreams", *The University of Kansas City Review*, XX (Winter, 1953), 113–120.

Deutsch, Babette. "Miracle and Mystery", *Poetry*, LXVI (August, 1945), 274–280.

Higginson, Thomas Wentworth. "Emily Dickinson's Letters", *Atlantic Monthly*, LXVIII (October, 1891), 444–456.

Howard, William. "Emily Dickinson's Poetic Vocabulary", *Publications of the Modern Language Association*, LXXII (March, 1957), 225–248.

Howells, William Dean. "The Strange Poems of Emily Dickinson", *Harper's Magazine*, LXXXII (January, 1891), 318–321.

Leyda, Jay. "Late Thaw of a Frozen Image", *New Republic*, CXXXII (February 21, 1955), 22–24.

McLean, Sydney R. "Emily Dickinson at Mount Holyoke", *The New England Quarterly*, VII (March, 1934), 25–42.

MacLeish, Archibald. "The Private World: Poems of Emily Dickinson", *Poetry and Experience*. Boston: Houghton Mifflin Co., 1960. pp. 91–114.

McNaughton, Ruth Flanders. "The Imagery of Emily Dickinson", *University of Nebraska Studies*, New Series No. 4 (January, 1949), 1–66.

Matthiessen, F. O. "The Problem of the Private Poet",

Kenyon Review, VII (Autumn, 1945), 584–597.

Miles, Susan. "The Irregularities of Emily Dickinson", *London Mercury*, XIII (December, 1925), 145–150; 157–158.

Moore, Marianne. "Emily Dickinson", *Poetry*, XLI (January, 1933), 219–226.

Moseley, Edwin. "The Gambit of Emily Dickinson", *The University of Kansas City Review*, XVI (Autumn, 1949), 11–19.

Sapir, Edward. "Emily Dickinson, A Primitive", *Poetry*, XXVI (May, 1925), 97–105.

Sherrer, Grace B. "A Study of Unusual Verb Constructions in the Poems of Emily Dickinson", *American Literature*, VII (March, 1935), 37–46.

Stamm, Edith Perry. "Emily Dickinson: Poetry and Punctuation", *Saturday Review*, XLVI (March 30, 1963), 26–27, 74.

Tate, Allen. "Emily Dickinson", *Reactionary Essays on Poetry and Ideas*. New York: Charles Scribner's Sons, 1936. pp. 3–26.

Warren, Austin. "Emily Dickinson", *Sewanee Review*, LXV (Autumn, 1957), 565–586.

Wells, Anna M. "Early Criticism of Emily Dickinson", *American Literature*, I (November, 1929), 243–259.

Wilbur, Richard. "Sumptuous Destitution", *Emily Dickinson: Three Views*. Amherst: Amherst College Press, 1960. pp. 35–46.

Wilder, Thornton. "Emily Dickinson", *Atlantic Monthly*, CXC (November, 1952), 43–48.

Williams, Stanley T. "Experiments in Poetry: Sidney Lanier and Emily Dickinson", *Literary History of the United States*, II. New York: The Macmillan Co., 1949. pp. 899–916.

Winters, Yvor. "Emily Dickinson and the Limits of Judgment", *In Defense of Reason*. Denver: Alan Swallow,
1947. pp. 283–299.
Zabel, Morton D. "Christina Rossetti and Emily Dickinson", *Poetry*, XXXVII (January, 1931), 213–216.

Index of Poems

❖

General Index

❖

180; references to illness and
death, 54-57; relation between
subject matter and form, 65-68,
102-103, 181-184; rhyme, 63-65,
182; royalty imagery, 95, 113,
166; on the silence of the dead,
80, 84, 93, 110-111, 115, 136-
137, 146, 152, 158, 163; on the
stillness of the dead, 80-81, 109-
110, 112, 156-157, 158; identification of time and death, 106-
107, 109, 123, 124; use of pronoun *it*, 80, 102, 111, 114, 158
Dickinson, Emily Norcross, 56,
140, 172-174
Dickinson, Francis H., 135
Dickinson, Gilbert, 170-172
Dickinson, Lavinia, 23-24, 57
Dickinson, Sue, 83, 171

Edwards, Jonathan, 36
Eliot, George, 170
Elizabethan Drama, 27, 28, 30
Emerson, Ralph Waldo, 48-49,
64, 146-147
Existentialism, 13, 32, 53, 80, 89,
101, 105, 108, 125, 126-127, 147,
153, 164, 176, 178, 180-181

Fuller, Margaret, 48

Garland, Hamlin, 21

Hawthorne, Nathaniel, 177
Hegelianism, 14
Heidegger, Martin, 13
Higginson, Thomas Wentworth,
18, 21, 26, 31, 41-42, 63-64, 127,
130, 138, 167-169, 172, 176, 182
Holland, Dr. and Mrs. J. G., 20,
22, 23, 56, 174

Holmes, Oliver Wendell, 64
Howells, William Dean, 21, 41,
54
Humphrey, Leonard, 19

Jackson, Helen Hunt, 174
Johnson, Thomas H., 12, 17, 31,
36, 58, 62, 68, 73, 80, 152, 154

Lind, Jenny, 44
Longfellow, Henry Wadsworth,
64
Lord, Otis P., 174
Lowell, James Russell, 64
Lyon, Mary, 46-47

McNaughton, Ruth F., 73
Melville, Herman, 58, 177
Mount Auburn Cemetery, 82
Mount Holyoke Seminary, 46-48,
50, 159, 177

Newton, Benjamin, 49, 176
Norcross, Frances and Louise, 59,
65, 96, 172, 176, 180
Norcross, Mrs. Joel W., 139

Parker, Theodore, 48
Perry, Ralph Barton, 37, 39, 41
Poe, Edgar Allan, 64
Puritanism, 35-41, 45-46, 49-50,
53, 74, 77, 99, 103-106, 124, 143,
145, 148, 159, 177-178, 182

Root, Abiah, 19, 55, 56, 82

Shakespeare, William, 28, 29, 30
Spencer, Theodore, 27, 28, 30
Stearns, Frazer, 59-60, 132
Stoddard, Solomon, 36
Synesthesia, 113